This page is intentionally left blank.

For information about this title or to order other books and/or electronic media, contact the publisher:

Resurgence, Inc.
info@resurgenceinc.org
www.resurgenceinc.org

Library of Congress Control Number: 2019938780

ISBN: 9781798534205,
         9781987041118,
         9781987045024

Printed in the United States of America

Cover photographs by Kamrin Tuerck

Jeff Wolf

RESTORED

YOUR MINISTRY CAN SURVIVE YOUR FAILURE

Published by Resurgence, Inc.

Loveland, OH

Contents

Restored

Your Ministry Can Survive Your Failure

JEFF WOLF

Dedications

This project has been more than two years in the making and wouldn't have been possible without the support of some key people. First and foremost, I'm thankful to the Lord for choosing me, being a patient Father with me, and never giving up on me. In Him I live, and move, and have my being.

To my beautiful wife, Christal, who has been my encourager and my rock. Thank you for loving me, supporting me, and sharing life with me. You are my delicate flower.

To my children, Kyelei and Seth: nothing has brought me more joy in life than raising you and watching you grow into the young woman and man of God that you are. Of all that I've done wrong, I must have done something right. I'm so proud of you two.

To my parents, David and Joyce Wolf, for laying the Godly foundation under my feet that would always sustain me when everything else crumbled around me. You are both models of Christian excellence, and have been the plumb line in my life (pun intended).

To the Resurgence, Inc. Board of Elders, Ken Angel, Rick Metzgar, Ken Wright, Rich Boll, Chuck Noel, Paul Dyar, Daniel Sturgill, and Terry McBeath, thank you for partnering with me. You all are examples of Godly husbands, fathers, and leaders.

Recommendations

"In your writing you are open and honest. You give encouragement and instruction to any pastor on the verge of burnout. I can certainly relate to so much of what you shared having served in pastoral ministry for 24 years. Experience can be painful, but is a great teacher. Everyone experiences some type of failure in life and ministry. You give hope to anyone struggling with failure."

-Pastor Gary Taylor (retired), Alabama

"'Restored' is a must-read for ministers. From the very beginning, you quickly become aware that you are reading the heart of a man who has been through the ups and downs of ministry. Ministry is rewarding, and yet can be totally debilitating. Before you make any big decisions about quitting, read this book. You will find out you're not alone, and that God has a plan."

-Pastor Adam, Virginia

"It's been said that gossip is saying something behind someone's back that you wouldn't say to their face, and flattery is saying something to someone's face that you wouldn't say behind their back. Pastors deal with both on a regular basis, and thus they often don't know who is really with them or against them. The end result is uncovered in great detail, and with great transparency in 'Restored'. I walked a lot of these painful steps with my friend, Jeff Wolf. The truth and courage required to experience a resurgence is now in your hands. You will never be the same!"

-Pastor Dan Sturgill, Jacksonville, Florida

"For God's gifts and His call are irrevocable."

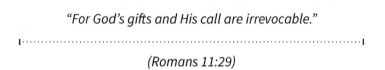

(Romans 11:29)

Introduction

A face only a mother could love, that's what I see when I look in the mirror. Every day, I am confronted with the reflection of a man who has made mistakes, who is not perfect, who wishes he could have some of life's moments back, who often second guesses himself, who has been hurt by people, and who has hurt people. No, I'm not looking for sympathy, I'm just embracing the reality that I'm human. I always have been, I always will be. I've become comfortable with that. I can work with that, and so can the Lord.

It took a while for me to realize that being saved and in ministry doesn't mean I'm no longer human. It means my humanity is redeemed by the blood of Jesus. I wish more people would get that. The truth is, a lot of people expect pastors to be Jesus. In case you haven't figured it out, pastors are not Jesus. He is the only human being that walked this Earth without sin.

Life has taught me that the world is full of cynical, judgmental people. Believers can be some of the worst. As unfortunate as that is, you are not as hard on me as I am on myself. I'm my worst critic. Most pastors feel this way. I have spent countless Sunday afternoons, over the course of ministry, beating myself up because I thought the sermon wasn't good enough. Many times, when someone chose to leave the church, I would spend days feeling guilty, racking my brain, and searching my heart to figure out what I did wrong. Pastors hold themselves to a higher standard than others hold them. Often, we feel like we're not measuring up to our own standards.

Sometimes, we struggle to give ourselves permission to be human, human enough to laugh at ourselves, human enough to be tired and need rest, human enough to cry, human enough to say "no," when there's too much on our plates, human enough to take time off, human enough to take care of our minds and bodies. The result can be burnout.

What you're about to read is a real, raw, and transparent look at the life of a bleeding shepherd, his struggle, and his road to resurgence. What this book is not is the chronicle of an unsuccessful pastor, the plight of someone who feels like a victim, or the quandary of a disgruntled has-been. I have nothing to prove. I believe with everything in me, there are pastors out there suffering in silence who need an advocate. I believe no one wants to talk about it. I'm here to have the conversation. My goal is that someone will realize, in reading this, their thought processes, feelings, and emotions are not abnormal. I want bleeding shepherds to be able to identify, and know they are not alone.

If you're reading this book, chances are you're broken. You don't need me to tell you you're broken, you are keenly aware of your brokenness because of the pain it causes. Other people know you're broken because despite your attempts to put on a mask, you've been struggling so long you've lost the ability to hide it. I'd imagine you've been surrounded by people who want to help but only seem to point out the obvious, like spectators on the side of the road, holding their faces, and pointing at a bad accident in despair. Spectators. It's not that they're not concerned or don't care. They just don't know what to do.

Can we agree from the start, we need the Lord to get in the middle of our brokenness and put the pieces back together again? Can we agree we need the Holy Spirit to breathe new life into us again? Can we agree prayer changes things and the anointing makes the difference? Since we agree, can we conclude we consider these truths to be a given in the equation of restoration, and talk about the down to earth practical things that affect us daily? I'm not going to spend time trying to prove how spiritual I am, but rather concede up front that it's in Him that I live, and move, and have my being, and without Him I am nothing.

With that in mind, I submit to you that you don't need one more well-meaning person to lay hands on you, sling anointing oil all over you, pat you on the back and tell you everything is going to be all right. You do need someone who's been where you are, fought the same battles, faced the same giants, climbed the same mountain, weathered the same storms, and has the scars to testify they made it through. That person will not just point you to the Healer, they will take you to the Healer. I'm that person. I've come to reveal my scars and be an ambassador of restoration.

If you're in ministry and feel as if you're headed for burnout or breakdown, please keep reading; I'm going to give you hope. If you used to be in ministry but have stepped away due to burnout, failure, or any other reason, I'm going to give you hope, also. I intend to convince you there is life after failure. If you're a family member, reading this book will help you better understand what's going on in your loved one's head and how to love and support them through it.

I want you to know, the following pages are bathed in prayer and compassion. This is my story and my testimony of restoration. Whether you've had a moral failure, left the ministry, been wounded by circumstances out of your control, or are just burning out and don't know where to turn, you are not alone, nor forgotten.

The enemy would like you to believe your ministry is on the rocks, but you're not getting off that easily. The gifts and calling of God are without repentance (Romans 11:29). One version says, God's gifts and callings cannot be taken back. Another version says, God's gifts and call are under full warranty, never cancelled, never rescinded. Yet another version says, God never changes His mind about the people He calls and the things He gives them. In short, God is not sorry He called you! Your deficits, shortcomings, and failures have not caught Him by surprise. He knew you before you were formed in your mother's womb, yet He called you.

Your destiny has never been determined by your deficits. Because we have created a ministry culture in which success is measured by comparison, we mark success by quantification instead of qualification. Quantification is the expression or measurement of something by numbers (quantity). You are not qualified because of the "numbers" in your column. Neither are you disqualified because of your deficits and failures. The enemy knows the unstoppable force that is the redemptive power of God. When he is unsuccessful in convincing you God *cannot* restore you, he will try to convince you God *will not* restore you because you've been disqualified. God is not deterred by your deficit. If necessary, He'll take you back to the potter's house and start over. So, stop beating yourself up!

Like you, I couldn't share my struggle with anyone when I was in the thick of it. I was afraid someone would think less of me or, my weaknesses would somehow be used against me. When you're a pastor, you're hesitant to risk exposing your humanity because you may lose the moral authority necessary to lead and shepherd effectively. I get it. I lived it.

If you're a struggling or fallen pastor, you probably have gone through a range of emotions, from shame to betrayal to anger, and everything in between. It's a roller coaster, and it's completely normal. You probably feel like no one cares. No one knows what you're going through. No one notices your pain. It's easy to make those kinds of generalized statements, but generalizations are the bait of the enemy to isolate you from the people that genuinely do see your pain and care for you, even if they're not sure what to do for you. The Lord isn't caught off guard by the struggle you're going through. He has already scheduled your divine appointment with an ambassador of restoration.

In keeping with Galatians 6:1, we have a responsibility to restore the broken. Of course, this wouldn't be a good inspirational book without a Greek word so, here it is. Katartizo. That's the word for "restore" used in Galatian 6:1. It means to mend, repair, complete, or fit together. It's also used in Matthew 4:21 where James and John are mending their nets. Additionally, Katartizo implies the act of resetting dislocated joints. When a pastor tries to lead in brokenness, it's proportionate to fishing with broken nets or walking with a dislocated hip. The result is hard work with no results. It's fruitless and pointless. Restoration is the answer, and restoration is everyone's business.

Now, there's a difference between *leading in* your brokenness and *leading from* your brokenness. I intend to convince you that brokenness makes you more effective in ministry, not less. The difference is the ingredient that turns your pain into your purpose. That ingredient is restoration. Someone who has walked through hurt and healing, failure and renewal, burnout and revival, is someone who's abandoned their idea that greatness is dependent upon perfection. In fact, the greatest people God ever used in scripture were messed up and had baggage. Restoration doesn't necessarily mean you have left your baggage behind. It can also mean God has taken some of that baggage and turned it from a burden into a blessing. I can't let go of everything in my past. I must take monuments of my past into my future so I'll remember from where the Lord has brought me.

In Exodus chapter 12, Israel didn't leave the land of their slavery empty handed. They took unleavened bread, they took flocks and herds and, most notably, they took the gold, silver, and clothing that was given to them by the Egyptians. They had to carry it out of their past, but the baggage was a blessing instead of a burden. God does not bring you through the battle for nothing. Your battle had an objective. Your pain had a purpose. As a result, you have grown in strength, wisdom, and maturity. That is exactly what makes you uniquely qualified to speak healing and life into someone else's brokenness. The most powerful statement you can make to someone who is wounded is, "I've been exactly where you are, and I made it through!" God has allowed you to be wounded deeply so He can use you greatly.

You've taken a bold first step. The Lord has connected us for a purpose. I'm convinced and determined we cannot afford to let another wounded shepherd die, including you. You can be restored.

"Besides everything else, I face daily the pressure of my concern for all the churches. Who is weak, and I do not feel weak? Who is led into sin, and I do not inwardly burn?"

(2 Corinthians 11:28, 29)

CHAPTER ONE

The List

I was a pastor. Pastors are people, regular, ordinary, imperfect people. We were born in sin just like everyone else. We threw temper tantrums as children, pushed limits, and received correction. We challenged boundaries as adolescents, drove our parents crazy, kept our mothers praying, missed curfew, got grounded and learned lessons the hard way. We skipped class in college, got speeding tickets, got our hearts broken, and stumbled here and there on the journey to becoming adults. There is nothing special about pastors. We just obeyed a call.

Pastors struggle with the same life issues as anyone else, such as depression, loss and grief, temptation, emotional baggage, health issues, family dysfunction, financial stress, and mental health issues. I've often said, I don't know how people navigate life successfully without a relationship with the Lord. When believers face these issues in their journey, they turn to the Lord and seek the counsel of their pastor, but to whom does the pastor turn when he himself is struggling? This is the question with no answer.

Yes, pastors seek the guidance of the Holy Spirit to survive, but just as believers need a shepherd, so do pastors need shepherds. Just as believers need someone to yield themselves as a human vessel to carry the Father's anointing, the pastor needs someone to be a human vessel, willing to be poured out so he may be filled up. Many pastors cannot find that person and end up struggling alone. Headlines like, "Prominent Pastor Commits Suicide After Battle with Mental Illness" are becoming all too common. What's worse is, we have heard it so often, we are somewhat desensitized to it and don't recognize it as the spiritual crisis that it is.

I'm not a statistician, but I am convinced for every pastor who has taken his own life, there are multitudes who have considered it. For every pastor who is struggling publicly, there are multitudes who are struggling privately. But why? For that regular, ordinary, imperfect person you and I call, "Pastor," answering the call to ministry was easy. Carrying the call is a different story. It's hard. No one says it better than the Apostle Paul.

"I have worked much harder, been in prison more frequently, been flogged more severely, and been exposed to death again and again. Five times I received from the Jews the forty lashes minus one. Three times I was beaten with rods, once I was pelted with stones, three times I was shipwrecked, I spent a night and a day in the open sea, I have been constantly on the move. I have been in danger from rivers, in danger from bandits, in danger from my fellow Jews, in danger from Gentiles; in danger in the city, in danger in the country, in danger at sea; and in danger from false believers.

I have labored and toiled and have often gone without sleep; I have known hunger and thirst and have often gone without food; I have been cold and naked. Besides everything else, I face daily the pressure of my concern for all the churches. Who is weak, and I do not feel weak? Who is led into sin, and I do not inwardly burn?" (2 Corinthians 11:23-29)

I've never been imprisoned, beaten, stoned, shipwrecked, lost at sea, robbed, without food, or without shelter and clothing (let alone Paul's other sufferings), but I know the daily pressure of concern for the church. I'm familiar with weakness and temptation. I have born what I felt was the weight of the world on my shoulders, and I buckled under the heaviness. This is my journey.

My story is anchored by three personal dreams, the first and last of which are separated by fifteen years. These dreams are connected and, ultimately, gave me a revelation into the most overlooked casualty of the war between righteousness and unrighteousness. Pastors.

THE FIRST DREAM

I dreamed I was in Cleveland, Ohio for a baptism service. After the service was over, I made my way to the parking lot. When I got to my car, I decided to go back inside to the men's room before beginning the several hours drive home. Back inside the building, I noticed I was being shadowed. You know, the awkward moment when you and someone else are walking toward the same door and are on pace to reach it about the same time. Do you speed up and get there first to hold the door open for the other person, or do you hang back and let them get there first? This seemed different, though. They were walking closer than what I felt was socially acceptable. It was just weird. I decided to pick up the pace and just get in so I could quickly get out. I rushed into the men's room, already planning my exit.

When I found an open stall, I went in only to be completely shocked that someone had crowded into the stall with me. To say I felt gravely threatened would be a gross understatement. I grabbed the person and demanded, "What in the world are you doing? Get out of here! Are you crazy?" Then I realized, this wasn't a person at all. It was the manifestation of a demonic spirit. Words cannot describe its likeness. The evil presence that swarmed that room was as thick as a cloud. Suddenly, I found myself in a fight for my life. I struggled with this being but couldn't shake it. I knew it wasn't a physical fight, but somehow I was fighting physically.

What happened next perplexed me for days to come. This demonic manifestation stabbed me in the arm with something. I saw it and felt it. It stung. I didn't know what it was, but it looked like a syrette, a needle that was used by combat medics in World War II to inject morphine into wounded soldiers. I felt something injected into my body, then the demonic spirit uttered these words, "Your name has already been taken off the list."

This utterance enraged me and I began to fight more tenaciously than before. I could sense the physical exertion; I could feel the blows of the enemy in my body. I fought until I prevailed and the demonic spirit fell visibly unconscious. Then I woke up in my bedroom crying out the name of Jesus and praying in the Spirit.

This was more than a dream; it was spiritual warfare in my sleep. It has happened several times in my life. These spiritual battles always come to an end when I speak the name of Jesus and the words transcend the sub consciousness of my dream, manifesting audibly on my lips into the atmosphere of the room, and I'm awakened by the sound of my own voice. When I opened my eyes, I could feel that same evil presence lingering in my bedroom. The temperature was cold in the room and the darkness manifested as physical heaviness. I persisted, pleading the Blood of Jesus until the evil spirit left the room.

I wish I could tell you the peace of God came over me, but instead, I was very troubled. This battle was different than others, this felt too real. Those words kept echoing in my mind, "Your name has already been taken off the list." What troubled me was, I knew what the list was: the list of people who God will greatly use.

That night, in the comfort of my own bed, the devil had come to declare a curse over me. He had come to tell me my dreams had been aborted, my vision had been erased, my calling had been invalidated, and my future had been destroyed. The devil's objective on that night was to convince me he had poisoned my life, injected me with the venom of failure and defeat, and I was done.

I'd love to tell you I never believed the lie, but the day came when I was convinced ministry was no longer an option for me. I felt disqualified and worthless. I abandoned my dreams and my vision. I turned my head downward in shame. But, thank God, that's not where the story ended! One day the Holy Spirit got a hold of me, breathed new life into me, and declared over me, "Your name is still on the list."

The biggest lie people like you and I have believed is, the Lord *won't* use us because of where we've been, but I believe the Lord *will* use us because of where we've been.

Take a look at this list. Noah was a drunk. Abraham was too old. Isaac was a daydreamer. Jacob was a liar. Leah was ugly. Joseph was abused. Moses stuttered. Rahab was a prostitute. Gideon was afraid. Sampson was a womanizer. David was an adulterer and a murderer. Elijah was suicidal. Jonah ran from God. Job went bankrupt. Peter denied Christ. Timothy had an ulcer, and Lazarus was dead.

That is the list of people who God greatly used! Noah built an ark for the saving of his house. Abraham became the father of Israel. Isaac was the child of God's covenant. Jacob wrestled with God until He changed his name. Leah bore Levi and became the matriarch of the priesthood. Joseph became the prince of Egypt who saved his people. Moses lead an entire nation out of captivity. Rahab begat the lineage of the Messiah. Gideon prevailed in battle with only a remnant. Sampson fulfilled his divine destiny despite his blindness. David was a man after God's own heart. Elijah never died, but God took him in a whirlwind. Jonah preached a revival and a whole city was saved. Job prayed for his dissenters and God restored double what he lost. Peter preached the first Pentecostal sermon. Timothy pastored the New Testament church, and Lazarus was raised from the dead.

That's the list I want to be on. It is proof, God will use you regardless of what you've been, where you've been, and who you've been. God will not disqualify you for His service based on your vices, your age, your maturity level, your speech, your looks, your wounds, your disabilities, your history, your fear, your crimes, your self-destruction, your disobedience, your financial status, your betrayal, your health, or even your life. If God will use these deficient, messed up, fragile, and broken people, then certainly He will do great things through you and me!

Ignore the enemy of your soul that has been whispering in your ear. Shake yourself. Reject the lie. Lift up your head. Your name is still on the list.

"Jesus straightened up and asked her, 'Woman, where are they? Has no one condemned you?' 'No one, sir,' she said. 'Then neither do I condemn you,' Jesus declared. "Go now and leave your life of sin."

(John 8:10,11)

CHAPTER TWO

The Revolution

IT'S TIME FOR A REVOLUTION

A revolution is a fundamental change in the way we think about something. When it comes to restoring burned out and fallen pastors, a revolution is exactly what we need. I wonder how many men of God are out there right now who were never restored. I wonder what they're doing. Perhaps they're selling cars, working in insurance, construction, or maybe serving as police officers. The truth is, when the enemy convinces you you're no longer qualified to be who God created and called you to be, you'll live your life in a crisis of identity. Maybe you're that person.

Why do we need a revolution? Because, hurting pastors are falling through the cracks. When we preach restoration but won't embrace our need for personal restoration, it's a sign we need a revolution. When a pastor gives his life to serve others but is left to wither and die when he himself needs help, it's a sign we need a revolution. When the conversion of sinners is celebrated but the fallen pastor is condemned, it's a big neon sign we need a revolution.

When the Pharisees caught the woman in the act of adultery in John 8, they brought her and threw her at Jesus' feet in front of the crowd (which is exactly where she needed to be, by the way). At Jesus' feet is where the woman was forgiven. At Jesus' feet is where she was restored. At Jesus' feet is where her purpose was renewed and her identity was reassigned. There was no better place for her to be, and there was an audience there to witness the miracle. But the Pharisees' motive for putting her there was not to position her for restoration, it was to position her for condemnation and punishment because that's what the law said should be done.

Jesus ignored her accusers, however, and spoke life into her, forgave her past, and spoke purpose into her future. He got down in the dirt with her and wrote her a note in the dust of the ground that was just for her, and said to her, "Go, and sin no more."

I've preached this passage countless times and have often wondered what Jesus wrote in the dust. There has been much speculation, but the only two people who will ever know with certainty what Jesus wrote with his finger are Jesus and the woman.

I've chosen to put myself in the story, to imagine myself sitting at the feet of Jesus humiliated, my sins and failures on display for the multitudes, my haters in attendance to watch me pay the price and gloat in their aura of self-righteousness. No false accusations, no trial, no denying it. I did it. There is no justification or mitigation to soften reality. What was done in the darkness has come to the light. I'm guilty. What would I be feeling? What would I be thinking?

Would I even be aware of Jesus' presence? That's an interesting question, isn't it?

Then one day, I found myself thrown to the ground, covered in the dust and ashes of what I once was, humiliated for my mistakes and failures. A has-been. And just like that woman in the Gospel of John, I saw a pair of feet. I don't know what Jesus wrote in the dirt for her that day, but I know what He wrote in my dirt. One word. Resurgence.

RAIN DELAY

This word, "resurgence", has been my lifeline since the beginning of 2017 when I went back to the pulpit for the first time in three years and fifteen days. It singularly describes what the Lord did in me after going through the darkest, most difficult season of my life. Resurgence is a revival, renewal, increase, or comeback. It is an action word; God's action of restoration in my life. In the pages that follow, I'll share my reflections leading up to pastoral burnout, contributing factors and warning signs, the stages of breakdown, the response, and a miraculous comeback story. I am the poster-child for resurgence.

I grew up in north central Ohio. We are Cleveland Indians fans by default. Naturally, I was excited when Cleveland went to the World Series in 2016. When they won three of the first four games, I was certain the Chicago Cubs would not win the three remaining games. I was glued to the TV for the rest of the series.

To my dismay, Chicago came back from a two-game deficit. The Indians and the Cubs went into game seven of the World Series, tied three to three. By the seventh inning stretch, the game was so intense I predicted they would go 10 innings. And it came to pass; I was proven a true prophet. At the end of the ninth inning, the game was tied at six. I was on the edge of my seat; Cleveland could not blow it now. Then something happened. It started to rain.

The rain delay at the end of the ninth inning changed the course of the game. What happened next, well, it just made me angry. In the tenth inning, Indians Pitcher Bryan Shaw intentionally walked two batters to load the bases. (This is when I began screaming at my TV). Subsequently, Albert Almora and Anthony Rizo of the Chicago Cubs scored two runs to make it 8-7, and Chicago won the game and the series.

In a post-game interview, Cubs General Manager, Jed Hoyer, called the rain delay the best thing to happen to the Chicago Cubs in the past 100 years.[1] ESPN interviewed Jason Heyward, who was responsible for calling a team meeting during the rain delay. That seventeen-minute meeting changed the outcome of the game. Heyward said. "Just needed to let these guys know they're awesome. Don't get down."[2] Whatever he said in that pep talk, it worked. The Cubs came back and won the game, breaking the proverbial curse on Chicago baseball.

It's game seven, the end of the ninth inning. The series is tied, the score is tied, and everything is riding on this. You're exhausted, you're discouraged, you're losing hope. You feel as if you are so close, but just out of reach of your breakthrough. Then suddenly, it begins to rain. The rain will cause a delay, but it's God sent. He wants to pull you aside, remind you He loves you, and give you the Word of encouragement you need to walk out on the field and get back in the game. The rain brings resurgence, and resurgence changes everything!

YOUR RESURGENCE BEGINS NOW

Despite the helplessness you feel at this very moment, you are always a candidate for restoration. Restoration is not about reversing the course of events that brought you to your present, it's about changing your direction. Corrosion can't be reversed; it can only be restored. If your journey is anything like mine, it is filled with tough days, insurmountable challenges, complexes of insignificance and inadequacy. But, don't look now; you're still here. You've made it this far. Make a conscious decision that your resurgence begins now.

To discount even one step of your journey, no matter how excruciating, is to discount the Hand of God that sustained you, the lessons you learned there, and the strength you gained there. Many years ago, the Happy Goodmans penned the lyrics, "I wouldn't take nothing for my journey now." Whether you like southern gospel or not, those words should resonate with you. Your journey made you who you are. Every step, every mile, every hill, every valley, every stumble, every pothole is significant in your journey. Each had a purpose and has forged its chapter in your story.

For the past several years, I have lived by four words: God doesn't waste experiences. Within seconds of reading those words, you have already recalled a bad day, wondering how God could've salvaged anything useful from it. At the risk of sounding cliché, I'm living proof God will turn your biggest mess into your most powerful message; one that is relatable to real people with real struggles.

That's why God doesn't reverse; He restores. The Lord told Joel, "I will restore to you the years which the swarming locust has eaten." (Joel 2:25 RSV). Reversal would remove the scar that reminds you that you were changed by the challenge. When Jacob declared, "I won't let go until you bless me," he was asking for the limp that would forever remind him of the struggle that made him Israel.

31

Jeremiah 30:17 says, "For I will restore health to you, and your wounds I will heal." (RSV). Do you know what happens when a wound heals? It creates a scar. Though it fades over time, a scar never completely goes away. It serves as a monument to an epic battle that made you a conqueror. Scars serve a purpose. Scars not only remind you of your victories, they show others you are not a novice. Scars show others you aren't afraid of a fight. Scars testify that battles are survivable. And by the way, when you are willing to reveal your scars, you give someone else hope for their restoration. Don't be ashamed of your scars.

I think people want genuine, so that's what I'm going to be. I have nothing to prove and no one to impress. I'm just an ordinary man upon whom the call of God rests. I don't claim to be an expert or a scholar, but I pledge to be honest with you. Writing this book required me to strip away what little speck of pride I may have had left and be totally open and transparent. You'll have to do the same to re-dig the old wells that have been clogged with "stuff", leaving you wounded, broken, and tired. The first step to your restoration is reaching out.

LORD HELP ME GET ONE MORE

We must change the way we relate to pastors who are burned out, have given up or have failed. We must identify the factors that cause a person, who is called, to quit or fall to temptation. We must become ambassadors of restoration, instead of spectators in the religious colosseum of failure. We need a new paradigm to bandage up those who are weak and wounded and refuse to leave them alone on the battlefield. We need a revolution. I don't have all the answers, but I'm determined to spread the conversation.

When I left the ministry, I wondered if anyone even noticed. I felt as if I had never mattered all. I discovered who my friends were; I also discovered who my dissenters were. The shame and humiliation of my failure were very real, but the Lord surrounded me with men of prayer and compassion. They loved and nurtured me back to health in the most difficult season of my life. Those few men assured me God was not through with me, that my worth and value had not changed, that my greatest days were before me, not behind me. They refused to let me die on the battlefield. They were my ambassadors of restoration.

I want you to know you're not alone. You're in a struggle, and I'm in your corner. I'm here to show you my scars, to be a living witness that restoration is not only possible but probable.

I have always been a war history buff. One of my favorite World War II stories is about Desmond Doss who won the Medal of Honor for his bravery on Okinawa. A movie was made about his life. He was a combat medic who was credited with saving the lives of 75 wounded soldiers single handedly in that battle. In an interview, the late Doss said, after carrying each soldier to safety, he prayed, "Lord help me get one more."[3] As I set out to be a spiritual medic to hurting pastors, I echo that prayer. Lord help me get one more.

"But you, keep your head in all situations, endure hardship, do the work of an evangelist, discharge all the duties of your ministry."

⊢ .... ⊣

(2 Timothy 4:5)

CHAPTER THREE

The Beginning

I was raised in a Christian home, by Godly parents who took me to church every time the doors were open. My parents provided a strong Biblical foundation in my life, which led me to accept Christ as my personal savior at a very young age. Mom and Dad were not just churchgoers. They were the real deal. They exemplified holiness and lived out their Christian witness, providing a solid example for my siblings and me to follow.

Family prayer was routine in our house. If we were sick, Mom and Dad called a prayer meeting before they called the doctor. If we made a mistake, they provided correction, forgiveness, and love and explained we should also ask Jesus for forgiveness. Mom and Dad didn't allow entertainment into the house that was in any way an affront to our faith. They guarded what we were exposed to. As does any family, we had our issues. Any family that looks perfect will tell you everyone struggles. However, regardless of our challenges, we were taught to love God, love each other, and do what is right. I'm very thankful for my Godly heritage and upbringing.

When I was fourteen years old, I felt very strongly the Lord was calling me into ministry. I was reading the Bible and the words of the Apostle Paul in 2 Timothy chapter 4 seemed to jump off the page at me. "Preach the Word... do the work of an evangelist." I let that sink in for several days. Not long after that, the Lord used my pastor to confirm to me what I believed was a definite call to ministry. One night, during the ride home from church, I explained to my parents what had happened to me, and that I was called to ministry. From that moment on, they became my biggest supporters.

I preached my first sermon when I was fifteen years old. Pastor J. E. DeVore, having recognized my calling, invited me to preach in a Wednesday night service. I was excited and terrified at the same time. I spent weeks studying, writing an outline, videotaping myself and watching it back, and making revisions. I prepared more for my first sermon than I believe I've prepared for any sermon since. When that dreadful Wednesday night service came, I took the pulpit and haven't shut up since.

Throughout my high school years, I became a student of God's Word. I read my Bible constantly, wearing out high-lighters and notebooks. When other teens were playing sports, going to school dances and being social, I spent most of my free time in my bedroom cultivating a love for the Word and learning how to communicate with the Lord.

I had aspirations of attending Bible college and entering full-time ministry. I strategically planned my sophomore and junior years of high school so I would have all but one class needed to graduate. I took the final class of my high school career, American Government, in summer school following my junior year, graduated with honors, and enrolled in bible college that Fall at the age of sixteen.

Looking back, I'm convinced my parents were crazy for allowing me to move into a dorm, on a college campus, more than five hundred miles away from home, when I was sixteen years old. As I write, my daughter is a senior in college and twenty-one years old. It's difficult for me to have her 350 miles from home, let alone when she was sixteen. Mom and Dad must have heard from God; they certainly had great trust in Him and in me.

Bible college was a great experience. I loved every minute of it and would do it all over again. During my college years, I met and formed friendships with people that have become lifelong colleagues. Of the five roommates I had in college, two of them I lost contact with, one of them is a real estate agent that I've stayed in touch with and one was a missionary to Central America. My last roommate, now a gospel recording artist, came to work on my staff for a season. We bought houses across the street from each other, were the closest of friends, and his wife was my insurance agent. My life has always been filled with those kinds of Kingdom connections.

During the last two years of college I served as a youth pastor. Back then it was assumed this post was the first step to eventually becoming a pastor. This was my first real taste of what local church ministry was about. I was no longer an outsider looking in, but now had the vantage point of those responsible for the shepherding of people. I was too young and naive to pay closer attention to what I was seeing. Regardless of my inability to fully grasp the value of that season in my life, it was a great experience, and one I will always have fond memories of.

Immediately after graduation, I was anxious to take the world for Jesus. If you're laughing, it's because you had the same thought when you were young and fresh in ministry. And you also know the feeling eventually goes away with your first dose of reality, leaving you with the sensation someone has punched you in the gut and knocked the wind out of you. That's where burnout begins to introduce itself.

I had a couple of opportunities to go into full time ministry as a youth pastor, but I felt something in my heart that went beyond local church ministry. I prayed and asked God to give me direction. What I felt strongly I was to do was, initially, not well received by those who loved me. I remembered the words of Paul to Timothy that the Lord used to alert me to my call: "do the work of an evangelist." I knew God was leading me into itinerate ministry.

During that time, in the mid 1990's, itinerate ministry was a completely different animal than it is today. The holding of revivals was still a regular practice among pastors of churches, large and small. If one had any lick of preaching ability, a strong enough network, a knack for public relations, and the ability to present himself, he could stay busy enough preaching revivals to make a living. While my family trusted my ability to hear from God, they were open about their skepticism, especially because I was supporting a wife and baby girl on the way. Perhaps this decision was the first I would make out of reckless obedience.

For a young preacher, I had a pretty strong network. I knew many pastors in my home state from attending and working youth camps and other state ministerial events. I had also networked considerably during my college years. I travelled with two different musical teams on weekends as a drummer. In that capacity, I went to churches and met pastors all over the country.

I set a launch date and used the time leading up to that to start working my contacts. I began by making a list of every pastor I knew, gathering contact information, and cold calling those pastors. I would share with them my vision and hope for a preaching appointment. It wasn't long before a few appointments snowballed into a five year itinerate ministry.

For those five years after college, I travelled an average of 40 weeks each year preaching revivals. The Lord blessed those few initial revivals I held and it resulted in a word-of-mouth chain reaction. My gift began making room for me. Eventually, I made very few cold calls because I was receiving constant invitations to hold revivals all over the country. I certainly was not a household name, but the Lord had blessed my obedience and continually opened doors for me.

My years as a full-time evangelist are very special to me. I reminisce with fondness upon the experiences, people, places, friendships, and successes I enjoyed in that season of my life and ministry. I would do it all over again if given the opportunity. After serving as a pastor for all those years, I still have a taste for the excitement of the evangelist.

When I was an evangelist I remember saying, "I will never pastor a church." Yes, I actually said it, multiple times. I was young, and obviously ignorant. My rationale was that I felt I was in the perfect will of God. I was having the time of my life blazing a trail, going from place to place, preaching like my coat tail was on fire. I couldn't see myself doing or being anything else. Obviously, God had a larger plan for me and I would soon see the bigger picture.

After accepting God's call upon my life, I experienced quick success early in ministry. That season lasted about a decade before my metal began to be tested. David also experienced early success. After being anointed by Samuel to be Israel's next King, David killed an untouchable, giant Philistine war hero with a sling shot! When he came of age, King Saul quickly promoted him through the ranks to become a commander of armies. It wasn't long before the women of the kingdom were singing David's praises above King Saul. Early, quick success.

David must have realized the futility of man's approval when things began to get awkward with the King. Saul tried to kill him, when all he was doing was playing the harp, and he eventually found himself in hiding. David must have thought to himself, "This is not what I signed up for. Where are the mobs of people singing my praises now? How did I go from being Israel's boy wonder to being a fugitive on the run, just trying to stay alive?"

If David's journey with God was depicted on a graph, it wouldn't resemble a vertical climb. David's journey was a series of victories and failures, sin and repentance, stupidity and wisdom. His steps forward were often followed by steps backward. But one thing was constant in David's life. God's love.

Acts 13:22 says, "God testified concerning him: 'I have found David son of Jesse, a man after my own heart; he will do everything I want him to do.'"

God vouched for David, God vouched for me, and God will vouch for you. Even after you have stumbled.

Denominations and religious organizations tend to measure the success of a ministry on a graph by nickels and noses. You and I are often expected to make the graph depict a vertical climb. While men are quantifying us, God is qualifying us. But in reality, our lives and ministries are like David's: full of sin and repentance, failures and victories, stupidity and wisdom. When we take steps forward, we will often suffer backward steps also. But God loved us, and knowing our weaknesses, called us and anointed us anyway. God has vouched for us.

If someone would have imparted this truth to me when I was young in ministry, perhaps it would've saved me a world of heartache, and perhaps would've detoured me from the road to burnout and failure upon which I would eventually find myself. This is not to say I had not been trained. I was raised by Godly parents, I sat under an anointed pastor (whom I consider my spiritual father), I spent four years at a prominent Bible college, I spent five years traveling the country preaching, and watching ministry. All of that was a pretty solid foundation, but none of it prepared me for sitting in the hot seat. I would leave itinerate ministry to become a pastor, and quickly realize I had stepped out of the frying pan into the fire.

Part of my induction into the pastorate was experiencing Godly humility. Having had such ministry success at a young age had caused me to believe I was pretty awesome, I'm embarrassed to admit. The Lord gently and lovingly lead me through some experiences that broke down my pride and resulted in a more accurate self-portrait. The more time I spent in the pastorate, the more my pride seemed to be chipped away. With humility comes wisdom (Proverbs 11:12).

MY FIRST PASTORATE

I was 24 years old when my daughter (3 years old at the time) asked her mom, "When's daddy going to come live with us?" It broke my heart. She had been on the road since she was born, but the older she got the more difficult it became to travel with her. I had to buy a luggage carrier just to tote all the baby/toddler equipment. I traveled alone for a couple years, until she melted me with that question.

So, I called the powers-that-be and expressed my interest in the pastorate. That's when I had my first experience of church politics. I went to a church of less than 100 people, in a rural part of Northern Ohio, on a Sunday morning to 'try out'. I've always hated that term, but that's what they called it when you went to preach as a pastoral candidate. I was up against another preacher who was well known in the state and had pastored for many years. I was sure he was a shoe-in. I just treated that Sunday morning service as if I were there to preach a revival. That was my comfort zone. We had a great service.

Imagine my surprise when the overseer called to congratulate me on being voted in as the new pastor. I was excited, but I was nervous. I knew how to preach. I had preached all over the country in churches up to a thousand people. I knew how to walk in my gift, but I didn't have the foggiest idea how to be a pastor. So, my plan was to 'have church' and figure out the rest.

Man, we had some good church; it was like revival every Sunday and Wednesday. We were even on local access television. For a while, I wondered why I hadn't tried this pastoring thing sooner! I was having a great time. (Yes, I know I was in my honeymoon. Don't get ahead of me). After a couple of months, I figured out having church isn't the only part of pastoring, and you can only go so far on good preaching.

I cherish the experiences I had and the relationships I formed there. We grew, paid off a mortgage, won people to the Lord and did some good ministry. Part of the reason my first pastorate will always hold a special place in my heart, is because my son was born there. That's where he was dedicated to the Lord. When the honeymoon was over, however, I got a taste of something bigger and decided to move on. That might have been my first mistake!

I pastored two more churches and served in state executive leadership for a while before landing in my 'Charles Dickens' church. I use that nickname because of the opening line of his novel 'A Tale of Two Cities', "It was the best of times; it was the worst of times."[4] My last pastorate gave me some of the best ministry experiences I've ever had. I look back with fondness at what the Lord accomplished through me during those years. Conversely, it also gave me the worst ministry heartaches I've ever had. I allowed myself to be defeated, I lost my vision, and consequently, my way.

"Strike the shepherd, and the sheep will be scattered."

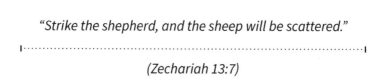

(Zechariah 13:7)

CHAPTER FOUR

The Nightmare

In 2005, I had the second most vivid dream of my life. Only a few times has the Lord used a dream to speak something profound to me, and this was certainly one of them. I awoke troubled, even afraid. It was hours before I could go back to sleep, as I relived every detail of the dream. The next morning when I woke up, I could still feel the heaviness of the dream in my spirit. I asked God to give me the interpretation. Over the course of days and months to come I shared the dream with a few close confidants, hopeful someone could give me some insight into what the Lord might be showing me.

It wasn't until years later I understood the dream's meaning. I was still young in the pastorate and burnout had never crossed my mind. I was somewhat of a "boy wonder" and felt invincible, having had quick and early ministry success. Never in my wildest imagination would I have believed the dream would be about me, my future, and my failure.

If you think the first dream I shared with you is crazy, listen to this!

THE SECOND DREAM

In the dream, I stumbled down a hospital hallway covered in my own blood. It was a long, empty hallway that seemed to have no ending. There were no doors, only sterile white walls and bright florescent lights that created a glare on the polished tile floor. I was unsteady on my feet, and bounced from wall to wall, determined to continue moving forward until I could find help.

I was suffering from a severe head wound, but didn't know what happened. I was all too aware every second counted because I was quickly losing blood, leaving a trail on the floor behind me. I came to the opening of another hallway and, rounding the corner, I ran into a group of people wearing white lab coats, huddled in the center of the hallway. I was sure they were doctors and nurses. I couldn't hear them speaking, but saw their lips moving. I suddenly felt a spark of hope I was going to make it.

What happened next still puzzles me. I crashed into the middle of the huddle, begging them to help me, assuming they would see my terrible head wound and the blood that covered me. I anticipated they would drop everything and begin to feverishly tend to my critical wound. I expected doctors to begin shouting orders and nurses to begin scurrying to supply closets for bandages, while yet others would lower me onto a cot and begin assessing my condition. To my horror, this did not happen. The people, whose meeting I had interrupted, looked at me with irritation and disgust on their faces. Rather than springing into action to save my life, they pushed me aside and continued their huddle. They acted as if they didn't see I was in trouble. They pretended I didn't exist.

My next thought was, these persons must not be medical professionals and didn't have the skills to help me. Even then, wouldn't they at least realize that, for the moment, trying to get me help was more important than anything they were doing? Wouldn't they run to get help? None of this happened. They completely ignored me. Why didn't they help me? I was stunned. I pressed on, searching for someone to save me.

This scene played out three times in identical detail. Each failed attempt for help left me more hopeless than the one before. Just when I was about to give up, I came to a set of double doors. I pushed my way through the doors and found myself in a large waiting room full of people. Chairs lined the walls and rows of chairs faced each other throughout the room. Every chair was full. I was sure the room would be filled with horror and concern at the sight of my gruesome wounds, but no one looked up. No one noticed. I was dying in a room full of people and no one seemed to care.

I would later live this nightmare in detail. Many pastors are doing the same. They're dying in a room full of people and no one knows. They're going through the motions. They're considering giving up. They feel like no one cares.

Research conducted by FASICLD (Francis A. Schaeffer Institute of Church Leadership Development) says, 100% of pastors surveyed had a close associate or seminary buddy who had left the ministry because of burnout, conflict in their church, or from a moral failure. 90% stated they are frequently fatigued, and worn out on a weekly and even daily basis. 89% considered leaving the ministry at one time. 57% said they would leave if they had a better place to go including secular work. 71% stated they were burned out, and they battle depression beyond fatigue on a weekly and even a daily basis.[5] These are not just stats; this is a reality! Congregations have ignored it, denominational leaders have ignored it, our families have even ignored it, and we wonder why we read headlines about fallen pastors. They need a resurgence; I needed a resurgence!

We need to wake up and take the scripture to heart.

Galatians 6:1-2 (KJV) "Brethren, if a man be overtaken in a fault, ye which are spiritual, restore such an one in the spirit of meekness; considering thyself, lest thou also be tempted. Bear ye one another's burdens, and so fulfill the law of Christ."

Zechariah 13:7 is the prognosis of a fallen shepherd.

"Awake, sword, against my shepherd, against the man who is close to me!" declares the LORD Almighty. "Strike the shepherd, and the sheep will be scattered." (KJV)

Perhaps you are bleeding right now and can closely identify with my dream. You may feel as if you're dying in front of a multitude of people and no one even notices. Perhaps you have asked for help but your cries have fallen on deaf ears. You may feel helpless, hopeless, and like you're about to lose everything. If you do, I want to encourage you; God has not forgotten you!

How could I have known the Lord was giving me a picture of what I would go through in the throes of ministry? My nightmare mirrors my experience in the height of burnout. I was bleeding; my head wound was indicative of my ministry and leadership role. I was aware I was in trouble, but I continued to stumble through the motions. I asked for help, in my own way, but no one seemed to recognize the severity of my condition. I was dying before a congregation full of people, but no one even noticed. At least that's how I felt.

At the time of my dream, I believed the Lord was allowing me to feel the pain and frustration of bleeding shepherds. I did not believe it was a warning or foreshadowing of something that I would personally experience, but it is exactly what I experienced. Today, however, the prophetic and practical significance of the dream is clear.

When the dream ended, the story had not ended. My story hasn't ended, and neither has yours.

"Carry each other's burdens, and in this way you will fulfill the law of Christ."

(Galatians 6:2)

CHAPTER FIVE

The Spotter

For the last several years, I have tried to keep myself in the gym regularly. For some, that may seem like a waste of time and energy and may not appeal to them at all. For me, it's a release. I enjoy getting in there around the muscle heads and doing my thing. I've also made some friends while tossing around the irons.

I haven't always enjoyed it. Going to the gym forced me to face my weaknesses, physically, mentally and emotionally. When I walk in the gym, and specifically the locker room, the sights, sounds, and smells trigger memories of junior high. See, I was the scrawny, awkward, diary-of-a-wimpy-kid looking person over in the corner, who was very uncomfortable and didn't want to be there. I'm an extreme introvert and I've never been an athlete. I've always been intimidated by almost everyone who showed even a shred of athletic ability in those settings. I was always the last person picked to be on a team. I was always the person the gym teacher made fun of. Yeah, that kid. Go ahead and laugh. I'm not that kid anymore. I've faced my weaknesses.

Going to the gym the first time caused me great anxiety. First of all, I didn't know what I was doing around all that equipment. Secondly, I was self-conscious that I would look like a fool, and thirdly, I was afraid I would fail. I was out of my element, out of my comfort zone, and obviously, out of my mind for putting myself through this mental and emotional torture, and paying $25 per month to do so. But I knew, to become stronger, I had to face and overcome those issues, so I sucked it up and persisted.

I did some research so I would know where to begin. I knew before beginning physical exercise I needed to stretch. Then I picked a weight bench and started out with just the bar, which weighs forty-five pounds. I felt weak pushing up that bar, as I watched other guys in there putting multiple plates on their bar. It seemed impossible that I would ever get to where they were. Over time, though, I added more and more weight until I was comfortable and confident putting forty-five pound plates on the bar, and doing ten repetitions with no problem.

Over weeks and months, as I increased the weight, I could see the change in my body and feel the difference in my physical strength. Being around those muscle heads also gave me ideas. I watched them work and picked up some of their techniques and tricks. As I grew in strength, I also developed good form, which prevents injury and maximizes muscle gains. In fact, I learned it's not only about how much weight you can lift, but about how good your technique and form were. Something else I noticed is, sometimes the muscle heads, that were capable of bench pressing 300-400 pounds, would lift just the bar, like I did when I started out. Why, though? I found that strong men lifted the bar without weights to refine their form and learn how to zero in on muscle groups before adding weight.

Pause and zero in on what I'm about to say. Strong men never stop doing the little things.

"Do not despise these small beginnings, for the Lord rejoices to see the work begin..." (Zechariah 4:10 NLT). This isn't a Bible commentary, so I won't go into an exegesis but I'll put the verse in context. God was addressing Israel's response to the foundation of the second temple. In short, the temple couldn't be rebuilt until the foundation was formed in meticulous detail. It's only logical that the foundation sets the tone for the finished project.

What I had discovered is, in the beginning, I had gone into the gym focusing on weight instead of laying a level foundation for building up my strength. I wasn't giving enough attention to form and technique. The result was, I was lifting heavier weights but I wasn't doing it with the correct technique and, therefore, setting myself up for injury. I hope you're picking up what I'm laying down right now. This is where somebody says, "That'll preach!" Even the strongest of weight lifters still give attention to the small things. When I started with only the forty-five-pound bar, I was so worried about appearing weak, I missed the opportunity to perfect my form and technique.

In Bible college, I learned the history and polity of the church, the academic basics of public speaking, the do's and don'ts of pastoral counseling and many other things, but I didn't learn to develop my form and technique. You can't learn that in a classroom; you must watch someone do it. Many pastors, including myself, start out focusing on being heavy lifters without paying meticulous attention to setting a level and solid foundation. As a result, we turn out pastors and church leaders who can preach the wallpaper off the walls, but struggle with conflict management, relationship skills, personal discipline issues, etc. In this way, a pastor or leader can look strong but in reality, he is struggling to hold up the weight because his form and technique is off.

If I had not surrounded myself with strong lifters in the gym, I would never have appreciated the importance of developing good form. As I watched them lift, and incorporated some of their techniques into my routine, I noticed it was easier to lift the weight. I also noticed, good form causes you to tap into smaller muscle groups often overlooked when you only focused on weight.

Now, when I go into the gym, I have no anxiety at all. I'm a regular. I'm surrounded by friends. I can perform my lifting routine and feel good about it when I leave. I'm not self-conscious, nervous, or embarrassed. I've conquered the fear of that adolescent, scrawny introvert. That's a place I had achieved in ministry, as well. I was confident in my preaching ability. I was surrounded by a staff that was competent and loyal. I was known in the organization in which I served. I was comfortable. When you get comfortable you will stop growing.

When I got comfortable lifting forty-five pound plates I stopped gaining. Two forty-five pound plates on a forty-five-pound bar is 135 pounds. That's nowhere near my body weight. Getting comfortable meant I wasn't "pulling my weight." I went to the gym for months and never put more weight on the bar. I would just work until I could do more repetitions in a set. My rationale was, I wasn't comfortable trying to lift more weight, so I would just lift my regular weight more times. Thus, I was working harder at what I could do comfortably, but I wasn't growing.

Again, pause and zero in on what I'm about to say. Many pastors are working twice as hard but not growing. A pastor who continues to do this will burn out.

There can be no analogy that more accurately describes what happened to me. I'm not afraid of hard work, nor am I afraid to tackle a challenge. I got to a place where I felt like I couldn't take on any more "weight" so, I thought if I worked harder I would get the job done. As a result, I became increasingly frustrated because there was no fruit. I was just spinning my wheels. I felt, no matter how hard I worked, I was not growing, the church was not growing, and the increase that I so desperately desired was not there. My form began to suffer and it all went downhill from there.

My error was, I allowed myself to become the strongest person in my circle. I was no longer surrounding myself with people who could stretch me or challenge me. There were no heavier lifters in the room to observe and learn from. Therefore, my growth stopped, frustration set in, and the burnout process began.

I learned another lesson in the gym. If I want to add more weight to the bar, I'm going to need a spotter. Remember, I'm an extreme introvert. Even though I had made some friends in the gym, I still didn't like asking for help. One day, I got brave and added twenty-five pound plates. That's an additional fifty pounds on top of my top weight of 135 pounds. I turned to a firefighter buddy of mine (whose arms are as big as my thighs) and said, "Hey, man, can I get a spot?" He replied, "Yeah, no problem." I told him I wanted to try five reps.

When I lifted that bar, I was nervous. It was heavier than I was comfortable with, but I wasn't afraid because I knew my spotter could help if I got in trouble. On the first rep, I brought the bar down to my chest, then pushed it back up. It was hard, but I did it. Now my confidence was increasing. The truth is, I had been strong enough to do it for quite some time, but I wouldn't take the chance on my own. The limit to my strength was only in my head. I could lift more, but I didn't know I could lift more until I did it, and I wouldn't do it because I hadn't had a spotter pushing me until now.

I pushed that bar twice more without help. On the fourth rep, however, it felt like someone had added more weight while I wasn't looking. My arms started to shake as I pushed with everything I had in me, but I just couldn't get there. I still wasn't worried because my spotter was there to help. He put his hands under the bar, but he didn't help me lift it. Instead, he started yelling at me to "push, push, push!" It motivated me to push harder! Then, I felt the bar begin to move upward again. I was relieved, as I assumed my spotter was lifting the bar for me. Once we got it back on the rack, he said, "You did it. I was only pulling about five pounds." Yeah, right.

He taught me a valuable lesson. The only way to grow is to increase your weight. The only way to increase your weight is to use a spotter and get out of your comfort zone. You will feel and see the results. Wow. So profound yet so simple. Today, I can put 185 pounds on that bar and lift it without a spotter, comfortably and with no fear. Once I can do that consistently, it'll be time to add more weight and call for my spotter again.

Every pastor needs a spotter. You should never allow yourself to be the strongest person in the room. It is necessary to stay close to someone who will challenge and stretch you to grow, do more, reach higher, and dream bigger. A good spotter is someone who is still spending time doing the small things well. A good spotter will encourage you take on more, for the purpose of developing your skills and increasing your ability. A good spotter will recognize when you struggle and encourage you to "push, push, push!" A good spotter will not let you struggle alone and will help bear your burdens when your arms are shaking beneath the load. A good spotter will always minimize his contribution and emphasize your improvement.

There's a reason pastors don't ask for help. We get intimidated by people who appear more talented, more charismatic, more anointed, more whatever. We often feel threatened by these types of people, and begin feeling terribly inferior and inadequate. Okay, maybe it's just me. A heavy lifter will tell you, he once walked into the gym and couldn't lift more than the bar. He will also tell you about the strong men he surrounded himself with that challenged him to become who he is today. So it is with giants of the faith.

One more thing, before I leave this analogy and move on. I was in the gym one day and heard someone calling for help. I looked over and saw this guy laying on the bench, struggling to get a bar off his chest. I quickly ran over and helped him get the bar back on the rack. He didn't have much weight on the bar, but it was more than he could handle. The gym was full, but I was the only one that seemed to see or hear him. I wondered why I was the only one who turned to help, but remembered everyone else in the place had earphones in and never heard his plea.

I give that guy credit for asking for help. It's not a big deal to ask someone to spot you, but it's pretty embarrassing to have to ask for help to get a bar off you. How ridiculous would it have been if he had just laid there on that bench, with that weight on his chest, for an indeterminate amount of time because he was afraid to ask for help? That's exactly what hurting pastors are doing. They've been under the weight so long, it has become the new normal. They've learned to live under the pressure, and cope with it in unhealthy ways. I give credit to pastors who recognize their struggle and reach out for help.

When pastors do reach out for help, we better be paying attention. It's easy to get so walled off in our own little world that we fail to recognize when someone around us is in trouble and needs help.

If you are on the bench, trying to lift more weight than you can handle, please don't be afraid to reach out for help. Letting all that weight sit on your chest isn't healthy. You'll hurt yourself. You'll burn out. Every pastor needs a spotter, the one who pastors a thousand people and the one who pastors a hundred. Even me. Even you. Don't do this thing alone.

My mission is to help you get the bar back on the rack. Stop trying to live under the crushing pressure of ministry. How? Here you go. Here's step number one. Remove some of the weights from the bar, until you get your strength back. I know that's a tall order, but scaling back is vital to your survival. You must learn how to delegate, say no, and let go of your superhero complex (regardless of popular belief, you cannot leap small buildings in a single bound). If you don't, you are risking your health, your family, your ministry and your sanity. It's just not worth it.

*"There remains, then, a Sabbath-rest for the people of God;
for anyone who enters God's rest also rests from their works,
just as God did from his."*

(Hebrews 4:9-10)

CHAPTER SIX

The Journal

Here's my honest confession. Pastoring is sometimes a dirty job and, unfortunately, I got dirty doing it. What I mean is, I got down in the trenches to fight and somewhere along the way I forgot who I was. Before I could experience a true restoration, I had to rediscover myself.

During the season leading up to my pastoral burn out, I was faithful to keep a journal. During my "rain delay" season, I pulled out those journal entries and began to reflect upon what I was feeling, seeing, and doing. Something powerful happened; I identified a pattern that led to my failure. While I was studying this, I began cross referencing my social media profile with my journal entries. It connected what was happening on a day to day basis to what I was writing in my journal. I was getting the perspective of an outsider looking in to a bleeding shepherd's life.

I found myself wishing the older, wiser "me" could go back in time, in some sort of time travel machine, and give the younger "me" some advice; to shout, "Wake up! Change your direction! Broaden your perspective! Choose your battles carefully! Don't give up!" As they say, hind sight is 20/20. Or, is it? Have you ever said something like, "If I knew then what I know now"? Well, what if you could know in your desert season what I know now after coming out of the desert? Wouldn't that kind of be the same thing? Keep reading.

This chapter is written out of a few of my most significant journal entries. It's difficult to relive these moments. In fact, it's quite emotional, but in doing so, healing comes. I pray, by sharing these intimate thoughts with you, it will impart into you a revelation that will strengthen your ministry and help you learn from my mistakes.

These journal entries are independent of each other yet they connect with an underlying theme: I was bleeding. I was bleeding in plain sight and no one noticed.

JOURNAL ENTRY ONE

"Wow! Another very powerful, encouraging, momentous Sunday! The attendance increased yet again today, the giving remains stable, and the people are excited. The tide is coming in, the church is growing, morale is high, and we're gaining momentum. This is what Pastoral ministry is supposed to feel like. It feels good. The pain had purpose, now it's time to enjoy the benefits of the purpose."

Reflection is both painful and insightful. I'm thankful I took the time to journal my thoughts on this journey, such as the words above I wrote on January 29, 2012. Having this historical first-hand account has become like a script for a season of my ministry. While it's painful to re-live the emotions of a broken-down pastor who was headed for severe burnout, it's also insightful to remember high tide moments like this. These moments were what kept the ship from scraping the bottom when I felt like I was about to run it aground.

The shallowest part of the channel into Boston Harbor is said to be about 38 feet during low tide. One of the ships that frequents the harbor, the Medi Nagasaki, has a draft of 38 feet.[6] Therefore, the ship can't enter or leave the harbor until the tide comes in. It's all about timing.

I once heard a pastor liken pastoral ministry to the flow of the tide; the tide comes in and the tide goes out. When the tide comes in, you ride it as long as you can. When the tide goes out, you look ahead and remember, the tide will come in again. From January to March of that year, I experienced a "high tide" season. It was a moment of peace amid the storm, but the Lord helped me get the ship into the harbor one more time.

Predicting tide tables isn't an exact science, naturally or ecclesiastically. It depends on countless external factors. So, how does a pastor know when the tide is rising in his ministry? The comment I wrote in my journal on January 29, 2012 that stands out the most is, "This is what pastoral ministry is supposed to feel like. It feels good." Pastor, have you ever made that statement? That's when you know the tide is rising. The Lord is giving you favor and making room to get the ship into harbor. I consider 'high tide' to be the season when you experience the tangible blessings of God, you are operating in momentum, you are making progress, the Lord is opening doors, and growth is obvious. That's where every pastor wants to be!

I remember that Sunday well. It was the day after my daughter's 15th birthday. I was preparing for Evangelist Joel Talley to come in town on that Friday for a three-day revival. Four days earlier, I had hit a large pot hole on a state route that had resulted in two flat tires and a broken tie rod. I had just shaken a migraine headache that had lasted several days. I was in the middle of basketball season with my 10-year-old son (his team was horrible that year). Life was happening, ministry was happening, I was keeping myself busy. But in all my business, I missed an opportunity. Yes, I was feeling good about what was happening, and it was a time of reprieve from a heated battle, but I didn't get the rest I needed when it was available; I felt it was necessary to work harder in response to what the Lord was doing, instead of resting in His strength and allowing Him to work.

As I stated earlier, I'm a military history buff. I also love good movies about warfare, whether fiction or non-fiction. One of my favorites is 'Crimson Tide,' about a nuclear submarine, named the USS Alabama (the actual 'Alabama' is a battleship) and its commanders and crew. There is a scene, near the beginning of the movie, when Gene Hackman and Denzel Washington, playing the Skipper and X.O., were on the bridge right before the boat submerges, watching the sunset. As they smoked their cigars, the Skipper turns to the X.O. and congratulates him for enjoying the view instead of talking it away.[7] When the Lord works in our lives and ministries, sometimes it's hard to step back, breathe, and watch His power at work. Pastors are control freaks and, therefore, have a difficult time letting go. When the tide comes in, the only way to capitalize on it is to enjoy the view, instead of talking it away.

It's important to gain strength and perspective from high tide moments in your life and ministry. They must serve to remind you God is moving in your life, even when you feel stagnant and fruitless. If I had capitalized on it by slowing down, regrouping and refilling, perhaps I could've ultimately avoided burnout. Unfortunately, I missed the opportunity. I wouldn't allow myself to pause and reflect, but worked to the point of exhaustion. This wasn't the only high tide moment I experienced in my pastorate, but it was the last before I would find myself at rock bottom.

JOURNAL ENTRY TWO

"Still living in the cloud from the authentic move of God yesterday. Every part of the day was amazing. The Lord is blessing our faithfulness, and we are beginning to see its fruit. I pray the Lord helps me, and gives me the wisdom to capitalize on the momentum of the tide that is coming in. I went to bed last night knowing the Lord is working. It's not that I doubted His working before, just that I wasn't seeing the evidence of it as I had wished. But now, God is manifesting His multiplication before our eyes. The seeds that have been planted in tears are bringing forth a harvest that we are reaping in joy."

Truth is, pastoral ministry is like riding a roller coaster at times. I don't like roller coasters; they make me nauseous and give me a headache. I don't find them enjoyable at all. My kids, however, love them. They live for the thrill ride and will get back in line to do it again. Ridiculous! When we go to an amusement park, I ride the bench. The bench is predictable, stable, trustworthy, and doesn't make me sick. I love watching how happy it makes them, but I don't want any part of it. That closely mirrors my experience with pastoral ministry. At times, it was exciting, at times it just made me sick to my stomach and I wanted to get off the ride!

I journaled this on February 6, 2012, just a week after my previous entry. I was obviously still contemplating the idea of high tide and reconciling several issues in my heart and mind: consistency, momentum, faith, sowing and reaping. It was a moment of reprieve in the middle of the wilderness. It reminds me of a similar season in scripture.

In Exodus, when Moses led Israel through the wilderness it must have been hot, dusty, monotonous and difficult, for Moses and the people. But the Lord didn't leave them without times of refreshing. When His people needed to be reminded of His promise and His presence, He sent the cloud to the tent of meeting.

Exodus 33:7-11 "Now Moses used to take a tent and pitch it outside the camp some distance away, calling it the "tent of meeting." Anyone inquiring of the Lord would go to the tent of meeting outside the camp. And whenever Moses went out to the tent, all the people rose and stood at the entrances to their tents, watching Moses until he entered the tent. As Moses went into the tent, the pillar of cloud would come down and stay at the entrance, while the Lord spoke with Moses. Whenever the people saw the pillar of cloud standing at the entrance to the tent, they all stood and worshiped, each at the entrance to their tent. The Lord would speak to Moses face to face, as one speaks to a friend."

God said to Moses later in that chapter, "My presence will go with you and I will give you rest." That's one of the keys to surviving a difficult pastoral assignment: Resting in His presence.

Looking back on my journal, it is obvious to me now, I was in dire need of that rest. However, like anyone with a stubborn work ethic, I always leaned more toward getting the job done and less toward pacing myself and conserving my energy. I would remain in the pastorate almost two more years before my burnout came to a head. I was like a locomotive, unknowingly headed for the end of the track, determined to go as fast as I could go. There was no one there to warn me I was headed for disaster.

When I wrote these words in my journal, I was right around the corner from a catastrophic derailment of that proverbial train. This is one of the last times I would write anything positive in my journal.

JOURNAL ENTRY THREE

"A trusted elder just came up to me and shared a Word. 'You are going to be a pastor of pastors; you are going to train pastors. This is your proving ground.' He has no idea the struggle I've experienced mentally and physically because of feeling like I've missed my moment. Thank you Lord for Godly people who will obey you when You give them a Word. I needed that today!"

Sunday, March 11, 2012. I remember exactly where I was standing. I remember the despair that had been setting in because of many failed attempts to follow what I believed was my purpose. Every time I tried to punch through the spiritual ceiling that confined me, I would find myself down for the count again. Each time I was denied, I lost a little part of my fight and resolve to prevail. Eventually, I came to the place where I believed I had missed my moment.

Here's what I want you to understand. I wasn't broken because I had not had good days or seasons of success, I was broken because I wasn't happy. I wasn't happy because I wasn't fulfilled. I wasn't fulfilled because my existence had been reduced to fighting fires. I felt like I wasn't building; I wasn't even maintaining. I was just trying to keep the ship afloat. I thought, surely, I had missed an opportunity to succeed, an opportunity to capitalize on my momentum and reach for the sky. I thought I had missed my moment, as if being used by the Lord in a great way was some sort of cosmic event that only occurs every so many years, and it would never happen again in my lifetime. It sounds dramatic, but it's exactly how I felt.

It wasn't always that way, though. Four years earlier, revival had broken out and lasted nine months. During that time people came from surrounding states to get in the flow. The Lord moved, the church grew, and it was an amazing experience. But when the revival ended, the real battle started. Anytime you press into the supernatural and experience a genuine move of God, hell takes notice. I wasn't ready for what came next, and I began a downhill slide.

That's why I'm thankful for small reminders like I received on this day. It seems to me God always places reminders of His promises along the journey. Just when you need it most, you see a sign that triggers your memory and God says, "I'm still here. I haven't forgotten about you. My plan still prevails." Realistically, if He revealed to us what we would have to go through to reach the fulfillment of His plan, we would probably shrink from the challenge of obedience. Our finite minds don't have the ability to look beyond the present struggle to see the ultimate plan and purpose of God. Therefore, He asks us to walk by faith, not by sight. When you lose faith, and begin relying on what you see and hear, you succumb to anxiety, frustration, fear, and feelings.

Walking by sight causes you to forget in the darkness what you heard in the light. When you walk through dark days, what sustains you is the Word of the Lord. I could begin quoting scripture after scripture that has been my lifeline in trouble and kept me moving forward when I wanted to quit. When I didn't have anything else to hold on to, I held onto the Word of the Lord.

The truth of the matter is, I had not missed my moment. You have not missed your moment. Your tomorrow is coming because He carried you through your today! Your tomorrow will be sweeter because He was present in the impossibilities of your today. Don't look behind you for the crescendo of your existence. Look out in front of you in faith, and keep looking until you hold in your hand what you now only hold in your heart.

JOURNAL ENTRY FOUR

"I have so much information coursing through my brain, it's hard to know what to write. I have been in an all-out fight for my life and ministry. The enemy is attacking me from every side. He's used people, peers, superiors, and complete strangers. But, I'm still here. I've asked the Lord to give me rest from my enemies even as Jehoshaphat had rest from his enemies. I know I will win. I know I will survive, but I need a break from the battlefield to be refreshed and renewed. I want my family to know me outside of the man who struggles to survive another day. I want them to see the real "person" that is beneath the layers of defense that I've surrounded myself with."

I had just returned from Gatlinburg/Pigeon Forge, where I had performed a wedding over the weekend. Someone had just informed me via Facebook, they were leaving the church (not exactly a stand up way to do this). Fifteen days earlier, I had missed a Sunday at my church to go "preach for a friend". In reality, I was trying out for another church and interviewing with their elders. Despite wanting desperately to get as far away from my current situation as possible, it didn't work out. Oh, well, I was getting ready to launch my first "I Love My Church" campaign, it would keep me busy.

That evening, I watched my son throw some pretty awesome pitches at baseball practice; he would strike out his first batter on the following Saturday. Instead of enjoying time with my son, I was agonizing over the thoughts I described in the above journal entry. I was overwhelmed.

You may be asking yourself, "Why are you sharing these private journal entries?" Well, believe me, they're being censored! Truth is, they give me insight, in retrospect, into the progression of my burnout. To share these with you is to sound an alarm!

When I wrote this, I was under attack. It was coming from all sides. Notice, I was asking the Lord for rest, not realizing He had given me the opportunity for rest, but I didn't recognize it as such. We're all guilty of that at some point; asking God for something He's already tried to give us but it didn't come wrapped in the package we had expected. I had a chance to go to the rear to be refreshed and renewed, but I insisted on staying on the front line. Thus, I was fighting exhausted.

It's obvious I'm a military history fanatic; you can see it in the analogies I used in writing this journal entry. I was describing myself as a foot soldier on the fronts lines, flanked by the enemy on all sides, unable to distinguish between enemy and friendly forces. I was running out of ammunition, I had no water, and I was covered in the blood of my own failures, in dire need of help.

Allow me to interject a short history lesson. In December of 1944, the Germans mounted a last gasp offensive against Allied forces. They were held back just outside the city of Bastogne, Belgium, which was being tirelessly defended by the 101st Airborne. The German commander, General von Lüttwitz, sent a message to the U.S. commander, Brigadier General Anthony McAuliffe, demanding surrender. McAuliffe replied with one word, "NUTS!" Despite being surrounded, the 101st held Bastogne until relieved by General Patton's 3rd Army.[8]

The siege of Bastogne was part of a larger battle, better known as the 'Battle of the Bulge'. It was one of the deadliest and most treacherous battles in World War II. The soldiers fought in frigid temperatures and zero-visibility snow storms. They lived, ate, and slept in fox holes dug by their own hands. They suffered heavy casualties from the exposure to the weather, as well as the merciless German artillery fire on their position. The objective of the 101st was to hold Bastogne at any cost. The personal objective of every soldier was to survive to do it again tomorrow. They succeeded in stopping the German's last advance and affected a turning point in the war.

I don't know what those soldiers went through in the foxholes outside Bastogne in December of 1944, but I know they must have been cold, tired, hungry, wounded and afraid. That's what I felt when I wrote those words on May 8, 2012. I was doing my best to hold my position, and survive to do it again the next day. Unfortunately, I felt like I was the only one on the battlefield. I needed a comrade to fight with me. I needed to know I was not alone.

You need to know you're not alone. If you identify with the words of my journal entry, you could be just around the corner from disaster. It's time to reach out and get the help you need. The 101st could only hold Bastogne for so long. If Patton and the 3rd Army had not come to their rescue, only God knows what the outcome could've been.

My friend, you cannot fight this battle alone, as I was endeavoring to do. It is the most demoralizing, hopeless, and lonely place I've ever been in my life.

If I had it to do over again, I would have gone to my most trusted friends and laid it all out; the good, the bad, and the ugly. I would have sought advice, mentoring, evaluation, and moral support. Had

I known what was around the corner, I would have done anything to avoid it.

JOURNAL ENTRY FIVE

"I'm at the end of my rope. Everything is coming to a head. All the problems I've been carrying are beginning to come crashing down. I sit here on this Thursday morning feeling the most helpless, hopeless feeling in my life, ever. I'm lost. I don't know what to say. I don't know what to do. I don't know who to trust. I don't know who to talk to. I don't even feel saved. Has God forgotten me? Have I strayed so far that I can't get back? I have no answers. I have no faith. I have no self-worth. I have no fight left in me. I'm tired, perhaps almost dead. Does anyone see? Does anyone care? Lord, why have you allowed me to get so low? Why have you allowed me to reach a place where it hurts just to wake up every morning and live? Why do I feel condemnation for wanting to take a break and get better physically, spiritually and emotionally? Does it make me a quitter? Does it make me a backslider? Or does it just make me human?"

Fast forward over a year. I was sitting on a hotel balcony, at 5:34 in the morning, overlooking the Atlantic Ocean, doing a terrible job of enjoying a family vacation. I was feeling guilty for taking time off because so many critical issues at the church needed my attention. I know what you're thinking, but I was programed that way. All pastors are programed that way. It's virtually inescapable.

What haunts me as I read this is that it was one of the last journal entries I would make before my burnout came to a head.

112 DAYS LATER

It was November 13, 2013. I remember it to be a cold, brisk morning. As was my daily routine, I got up and went to the gym.

My workout routine consisted of about ten minutes of cardio and some weight training. While working on the Olympic bench, I felt a pinch in my chest. I assumed I had overdone it a little and backed off. I went on to finish my workout with some cardio and started to feel tired and dizzy. Again, I assumed I had overdone it and it was time to go home.

I walked out of the gym, and went into Walgreens next door to pick up a prescription for one of the kids. I rounded the corner in the card isle and ran into Keith, a police sergeant, fellow believer and friend. He and I stood there and talked a few minutes; he was telling me he had been off work for a few weeks following a training injury. I remember the conversation like it was yesterday. I also remember how I felt. I started to break out in a cold sweat. I was dizzy, nauseous, and felt as if the room was closing in on me. I was trying very hard to conceal what was suddenly happening in my body, but Keith recognized something was off and said, "You don't look so good, brother. Are you okay?" I fessed up immediately, and admitted I felt bad suddenly and needed to sit down before I passed out and fell.

I sat down on the floor right there in the greeting card isle in Walgreens. Keith didn't hesitate to act, he got on his radio and called for EMS. I explained to him, I had just left the gym and I thought I had overdone it. I would have been embarrassed except, I felt too horrible to care. The employees brought me some water and I sat there fighting off the feeling I was going to faint, while Keith talked to me. After a few minutes, I felt better, but still lousy.

The paramedics showed up and I gave them the typical male response that I was okay, just worked too hard at the gym and I didn't need to go to the hospital. One of the medics said, "I'll make you a deal; come out to the squad and let me put you on the monitor. If everything looks good, we won't make you go to the hospital." I agreed. When they put me on the monitor, the medic looked at the screen for a few seconds and then said something I never thought I'd hear, at least not at 38 years old, "You're having a heart attack. We're taking you to the hospital." Within an hour of the paramedic's words, I was in the heart cath lab getting two brand new stents installed.

When I came out of recovery, I was placed in intensive care. If you've ever gone through this, you know the drill. I had to lay flat on my back for six hours and my blood clotting numbers had to reach a certain level before the catheter port could be removed from my femoral artery. When the nurses came in to remove it, they explained that once the port was removed, the next step would be to apply direct pressure to the insertion sight for a minimum of twenty minutes, to ensure my blood clotted properly and the artery was sealed. When they began the process, everything seemed to be going smoothly. The pain was intense for several minutes, as a nurse applied direct pressure, meaning she put all her weight on my artery. Suddenly, I became very sick; the room started to spin, I became dizzy and light-headed, and tunnel vision set in, then everything went black.

After what seemed like a second, I came to, and opened my eyes to a chaotic sight. The room, which was only occupied by two nurses and me when I blacked out, was now full of nurses and doctors including one straddling my bed (apparently, who had been pumping my chest), and one saying in my ear, "everything is going to be okay." I began to ask what happened and no one would tell me. After I persisted, a nurse finally told me my heart had stopped for approximately 60 seconds. I have never been so afraid in my life.

My eyes filled with tears, as they brought my family in to ensure them I was okay. This experience triggered an anxiety in me I had never had: the fear of dying.

When I journaled those words on July 25th, I felt very helpless, but I never imagined 112 days later I would have a heart attack, at 38 years old. I don't know what I could say to you at this very moment to make my message to pastors any clearer. I want you to reflect on these words, "Jesus already died for the church; there's no need for you to kill yourself trying to pastor it." That's what a trusted confidant said to me while I was recuperating from this life changing experience.

SABBATICAL

If ministry is killing you, literally, like it almost killed me, you need a sabbatical. More than three months earlier, I recognized the need and requested a three-month sabbatical from my state bishop. When I had the heart attack, I had already been on sabbatical for almost two months. I had been taking care of myself and eating right for almost a year. So, my biggest question to the cardiologist was, "why?" He said, my only two risk factors were family history and stress (although, he could not wrap his mind around how ministry could possibly be so stressful that it could drive someone to cardiac distress. I replied, he was looking at clinical proof.)

Yes, I'm telling you, I was healthy, exercised regularly, ate right, had a body mass index less than 20 percent and had a heart attack anyway. Why? Because the stress of a difficult pastorate had worn me down physically to the point of heart failure. The sabbatical was too little, too late. If I had requested and taken a sabbatical and got the help I needed much earlier, it may have altered this course of events. That's a question I'll never have the answer for.

Until just a few years ago, sabbaticals were thought to be reserved for professors who took a semester off to study abroad. We had never heard of such a concept in ministry. Fortunately, ecclesiastical organizations are opening their eyes to the problem and adopting preventative and emergency sabbatical plans.

My purpose here is not to explain, justify or defend sabbaticals but to share my personal experience and belief in their value. There are plenty of resources out there to educate you, one of which is soulshepherding.org. If you believe you need a sabbatical, do your homework, create a plan and go to your leaders.

JOURNAL ENTRY SIX

Fast forward about four years. I wrote the following on June 2, 2017, three years, four months, and 24 days after I left the pastorate at the culmination of my burnout. I was healing. I was preaching again. I was living with peace in my heart, for the first time in a long time. But, I was still haunted by some of the emotions of the past.

"I still struggle with some of the factors that contributed to my burnout. Take today, for instance. It was a normal day; a day off before a long weekend ahead of me. I got up and went to the gym for a while, then spent most of the afternoon sitting in my recliner, drinking coffee, watching TV, perusing Facebook; basically just chilling out. Out of nowhere, a feeling of guilt gripped me! I felt guilty for resting; guilty for not doing something "productive!" How ridiculous is that?

That feeling was a mental flashback to pastoral ministry. I'm willing to bet, every pastor reading this immediately identified with that feeling. Why? Because we are all cut from the same cloth. Pastors, at least successful ones, are servants. I would even argue, no one is called or drawn into the pastorate without a deep sense of servanthood. The issue is, servants have a hard time giving themselves permission to rest. Servants, and therefore pastors, struggle with saying, "No."

Pastors often expect too much of themselves. Subsequently, people will begin to expect from a pastor what he expects of himself: too much! Have you ever seen the old circus act where the performer would spin a plate on a broom handle? After the first plate was spun, he would begin to add more plates to more broom handles. By the time the sixth or seventh plate was spun, the first was starting to wobble and the performer would run back over and spin the plate again. As a pastor, I always had several plates spinning and inevitably one of them was always wobbling and needed to be spun again. There was no time for rest!

As a pastor, I always set out to take Mondays off. After a busy Sunday, I was spent and needed to recharge. Despite my best intentions, I would always find myself working on something that was dominating my thoughts. I couldn't shut it off. I felt guilty for taking a day off. I was afraid one of the plates would stop spinning, fall, and break! Unfortunately, I allowed this guilt, this condemnation, all too often to steal my rest seasons, to my detriment.

Perhaps part of the problem was, I viewed myself as a lone ranger; no one could do it better than me. This was in spite of the fact that I had paid staff members that were competent and could handle anything I threw at them. It wasn't that I didn't trust them to watch the flock, it was my inability to turn off the plate spinner inside me. And eventually, I paid the price.

If you're a pastor, you must give yourself permission to rest. Schedule a day or two off every week and guard it strictly. Not everything is an emergency. Learn to triage situations that arise instead of treating everything and everyone as a life or death case. It's okay to block out time to do nothing. Lay on the couch, make popcorn and watch a movie. Sleep in. Walk around the mall with your wife. Play a round of golf, hunt or fish. Do something unproductive and do it regularly. It's okay.

Today, following that momentary flashback of guilt, I quickly remembered, today was my day off and I didn't owe anyone an explanation for how I spent my time. I work hard, and it's okay to let my mind and body get the rest it needs."

Hebrews 4:9-10 "There remains, then, a Sabbath-rest for the people of God; for anyone who enters God's rest also rests from their works, just as God did from his."

"Where no counsel is, the people fall: but in the multitude of counsellors there is safety."

(Proverbs 11:14)

CHAPTER SEVEN

The Factors

I've done my research. There is a multitude of materials out there about ministry burnout. For me, experience has outweighed my research.

Now, keep in mind I do not claim exclusivity when it comes to identifying the factors that contribute to ministry burnout. In fact, every pastor who has had the experience could probably write a list of factors of his or her own. What I've included in this chapter are a few of the factors that are most relevant to my experience. I am no expert, just a regular guy who allowed ministry to get to me, and ultimately, break me down.

I am not a clinical psychologist or counselor. I am not qualified to diagnose you, nor am I presuming to insist you are headed for burnout if you identify with my thoughts. I only want to give you some warning signs.

There's a spot in downtown Cleveland where I-90 makes a ninety-degree right turn (otherwise, you'd end up in Lake Erie). Clevelanders call it Dead Man's Curve because it is said to be the deadliest roadway in the city. Many people over the years have ignored the warning signs, "Curve Ahead, Slow Down", and it ended in tragedy. The Ohio Department of Transportation has rolled out many safety measures, over the years, to reduce accidents including, lowering the speed limit to 35, banking the curve, and installing extra signage and rumble strips. Nevertheless, people still ignore the signs.

I ignored the signs of burnout. Perhaps, I didn't even clearly recognize the signs. As I look back, it is now clear that if I had read the signs, I could've possibly avoided the crash. You don't have to consider me an expert by any stretch of the imagination. I'm just asking you to read my signs. If you identify with only one, it will have been worth every minute I've worked to share my story.

BETRAYAL

Psalm 55:12-14 "For it is not an enemy who reproaches me; then I could bear it. Nor is it one who hates me who has exalted himself against me; then I could hide from him. But it was you, a man my equal, my companion and my acquaintance. We took sweet counsel together, and walked to the house of God in the throng."

Psalm 41:9 "Even my own familiar friend in whom I trusted, who ate my bread, has lifted up his heel against me."

David's words throughout the Psalms most definitely come out of his own experiences; his experiences with man contrasted with his experience with God. When he wrote the above 2 passages, he did so as one who knows the pain of being betrayed by a friend.

Betrayal has to be one of the most devastating steps of pastoral burnout. Take the dynamic a step further and realize David is speaking of his friends. He's not speaking of those whom he pastored. A friend expects at least a little reciprocation of his friendship. A pastor often ministers to those who can do nothing for him in return. To be betrayed by a friend is painful, but to be betrayed by someone, to whom you've always given and asked nothing in return, is death.

When a pastor goes through betrayal, it may be the first blow to his ideal perception of ministry. It's ideal that everyone shows a level of respect to the ministry, that those who sit under a pastor's ministry love him or her and their family, that a congregation will follow a pastor's vision without question because he or she has the purest of intentions at heart. That's ideal, but pastoral ministry is anything but ideal.

Betrayal raises its ugly head early in ministry. I had my first taste at the ripe young age of 26 as a new pastor. It followed me all the way to burn out. I'll talk about this in greater detail later. Unfortunately, I don't believe there's any way to avoid betrayal in ministry, you just have to prepare yourself for it and respond and react appropriately. Some hard lessons are learned when betrayal is the teacher.

BURNING FIELDS

2 Samuel 14:29,30 "Therefore Absalom sent for Joab, to send him to the king, but he would not come to him. And when he sent again the second time, he would not come. So he said to his servants, "See, Joab's field is near mine, and he has barley there; go and set it on fire." And Absalom's servants set the field on fire."

Absalom. He was one of the sons of King David. He had his brother, Amnon, killed to avenge the disgrace of his sister, Tamar. When King David heard the news, he mourned the loss of his son, and Absalom fled. Three years later, the King allowed Absalom to return to Israel, but wouldn't see him for another two years. Meanwhile, Absalom plotted a conspiracy to overthrow the throne. The Bible said, he stole the hearts of the men of Israel.

After two years had passed, Absalom decided he was going to attempt to see his father. He sent for Joab, captain of David's army, to request to see his Father. Joab refused to answer. He tried a second time and Joab refused again.

This is when Absalom decided to get Joab's attention. He had his barley field set on fire. The barley harvest was ripe and Absalom destroyed it. It worked. Joab took the message to King David.

Pastors, at some point in your ministry, you will deal with an Absalom. This is the person who will cause you grief at the expense of the harvest. Unfortunately, for most pastors, a name came to mind as you read this. The Absaloms in your path, if not dealt with, will push you closer to burnout.

The reason this is important is, the Scripture shows us what happens when Absalom isn't properly dealt with, or just flat ignored. Absalom is the man that eventually drives King David off his throne, out of his palace, into the wilderness and running for the hills for his own safety. Absalom displaces proper authority. Absalom misdirects trust and loyalty. Absalom has the ability to manipulate people into believing a lie. Absalom is rebellious, unrepentant, and quite frankly, a sociopath.

As a pastor, you will deal with one Absalom after another in your ministry. If you let it go unchecked, it will become like a torpedo speeding headlong into the hull of the ship, just below the surface, and it will wreak havoc and destruction upon your ministry, and upon you personally. The spirit of Absalom wants to destroy your success, your confidence, your integrity, your reputation, your ministry and everything you are working hard to accomplish.

The best way to deal with Absalom is to keep him close. Have you heard the saying, "Keep your friends close and your enemies closer?" I'm not suggesting anyone in your congregation is the enemy. I'm saying if you identify an Absalom in your congregation, keep them close to you. Keep the lines of communication open. Kill them with kindness without letting your guard down and, most of all, seek the Lord's direction. This battle can only be won by prayer and intercession.

Don't let Absalom burn your field and destroy your harvest.

UNREALISTIC EXPECTATIONS

Acts 13:22 says, "God testified concerning him: 'I have found David son of Jesse, a man after my own heart; he will do everything I want him to do.'"

God identified in David what I call reckless obedience. He said, "He will do everything I want him to do." Reckless obedience means, obeying God regardless of the fallout. That's what David always did. God also knew, while David would always obey Him, he would do some things the wrong way. David had some reckless disobedient moments, too. Yet, despite all of David's faults, imperfections, and mistakes, God knew David's heart was His, and His heart was in David. God expected David to sin and repent, fail and succeed, lose and win, make mistakes and learn from his mistakes. God expected David to be human, but to continually turn his heart toward Him, and walk in obedience.

One of the worst enemies of today's pastors is unrealistic expectations. Pastors seem to be expected to be nothing short of super-human. We are expected to be everywhere at once, to be all things to all people, to know all the answers, to make every hospital visit, to answer every phone call, to be in the office 60 hours a week, to say the right thing every time, to preach our best sermon every Sunday, to pray hours a day, fast forty days a month, to be involved in every civic activity, and still find time for our families. Those expectations, all of which come from people, are unrealistic. No human being can do all of that all the time. Yet, pastors find themselves pursuing those expectations and beating themselves up with guilt and condemnation when they can't accomplish it all!

Pastors, without healthy boundaries in your life, you will succumb to the vicious cycle. You are doing yourself a disservice by trying to live up to every expectation thrust upon you by your congregation. Say nothing of the fact that you are setting up your successor for failure. I followed a pastor who thought he was Superman; he tried to do everything up to and including leaping small buildings with a single bound. Don't get me wrong, he is a great pastor and a great man. Then I came along and took it on the chin because I had different boundaries. I was already a failure because I wasn't him! Do you see my point?

Boundaries help you to maintain your priorities. If you don't set clearly defined boundaries and insist they be respected, you will put yourself on the fast track to burnout. Guard yourself against unrealistic expectations. It just may save your ministry.

THE ABSENCE OF WISE COUNSEL

Proverbs 11:14 "Where no counsel is, the people fall: but in the multitude of counsellors there is safety."

I recently read a blog post by Tim Enochs. He said this: for every single degree you fly off course, you will miss your target landing spot by 92 feet for every mile you fly. That amounts to about one mile off target for every sixty miles flown. If you decided to start at the equator and fly around the earth, one degree off would land you almost 500 miles off target.[9] So, the longer you travel off course, the further you will be away from the intended target.

A pilot wouldn't fly without the informational input provided by his radar. You and I, especially in ministry, shouldn't navigate our journey without wise counsel from trusted advisers.

Question: What could've prevented me from getting burned out? What could I or anyone else have done to correct the problem before it started?

Answer: If I had sought out someone ten years my senior in experience and asked them to evaluate my life and ministry, and had I made their suggested small course corrections ten years ago, I would likely be in a different place today. Small course corrections early on can keep your vision intact and preserve the integrity of your destiny. Being one degree off ten years ago, if left uncorrected, will result in your being hundreds or even thousands of miles off today.

The key here is wise counsel must be "sought out." Pastors don't like to ask for help because they fear their weaknesses will be exploited against them. If you feel like you're off course, find someone you trust, someone who is wise, and ask for help! There's no shame in asking for help. You may be surprised to find out, you're in good company!

Psalm 1:1-2 "Blessed is the man who walks not in the counsel of the ungodly, nor stands in the path of sinners, nor sits in the seat of the scornful; but his delight is in the law of the Lord, and in His law he meditates day and night."

My wife's car has this new technology called, 'lane departure assist.' There's a tiny camera built into the back of the rear-view mirror that reads the lines on the road. When it senses the car is crossing the line, it gives you this very annoying beeping alarm, and the steering wheel begins fighting you and correcting your course. The only way to overcome this safety feature is to use your turn signal. It's very annoying if you aren't in the habit of using your turn signal.

Isn't that kind of how the Holy spirit works? He knows the path and direction you're going; when you begin to go off center, He begins nudging you to correct your course.

*"Though one may be overpowered, two can defend them-
selves. A cord of three strands is not quickly broken."*

(Ecclesiastes 4:12)

CHAPTER EIGHT

The Course Corrections

Someone asked me, "If you could go back in time, what are some course corrections you would've made?" I could've done a better job in many areas. I'll share four things. It's not that I wasn't doing them, I just could've done better. I call them the 4H's.

1. Guard your heart.

2. Guard your health.

3. Guard your head.

4. Guard your home.

As a pastor, I learned that making major shifts in the operation of the church is often too much change for people to handle. People don't like change. People will oppose and fight change. In my experience, you can accomplish the same goals by making small course corrections. They add up to the significant shift you're looking for.

The same is true in your pastoral ministry. When you've operated a certain way as a pastor, it's difficult to change. You may not have one large issue that is carrying you off course. It may be a dozen little things that add up to something that will cause you to miss your mark in the long run. Making small course corrections in your personal and professional life can make a huge difference.

GUARD YOUR HEART

What would I do differently? First, I would do a better job of guarding my heart. When the factors of burnout begin to surface, it's easy to become jaded by the disappointment and betrayal you feel. If you aren't guarding against it, you can develop a callous on your heart. Hard hearts begin with one callous. I know it's hard to swallow when you feel betrayed by people you trusted, and it's easy to allow the seed of bitterness to be planted. It may seem like only a small dislike for someone, and it seems so justifiable when someone has done you wrong, but over time, that small callous will harden your heart to people, and can affect your relationship with the Lord and even hinder your prayers!

Guarding your heart means rejecting the temptation to give in to ill feelings, idle speech, gossip, and unforgivingness. I really want you to meditate on this because it's present in all of our lives. Has someone offended you, hurt you, rubbed you the wrong way, got under your skin and you would rather not be around them? That's the person you need to think about for a moment. Is your clash with this person a simple personality conflict, or is it deeper? How do you know the difference? Ask yourself a series of questions. When you see this person, do you intentionally avoid them? Do you cringe when you hear their name? Do you engage in gossip of which this person is the subject? If you answered "yes" to any of those questions, you have allowed a callous to form on your heart.

Let me just say this, it's impossible to go through the pastorate without the temptation to have ill feelings against someone to whom you've ministered at some point or another. Not one member of your congregation is perfect. You are going to feel betrayed along the way. But the health of your heart is more important than the size of your ego. Being justified to be angry with someone doesn't make it okay to stay angry with them. Would you rather be right, and risk your heart being calloused, or would you rather be free?

Several years ago, another pastor and I had a difference of opinion. The "why" is irrelevant. I avoided him at state meetings, I rolled my eyes when someone mentioned him and I cringed when I heard his name. I had allowed my heart to become hard toward him. One summer night, I found myself sitting in front of him at a camp meeting service. I went through the whole service feeling as uncomfortable as you can imagine. Afterwards, the Holy Spirit whispered into my ear, instructing to me go to this pastor and make things right.

Now, let me impress upon you, I felt justified in my dislike of him. I felt he had done me wrong. I knew, however, that didn't matter and it was time to deal with it. I walked up to that pastor, looked him in the eye and asked him to forgive me for harboring bitterness against him. The two of us and Jesus got our business fixed right then and there. I cannot put into words the sense of relief and freedom I felt when I walked out of the place! When you get free from the callouses that have developed on your heart, answers to prayer begin to unlock, doors begin to open, anointing begins to flow. All those things are stalled when you allow your heart to be affected by your differences. Today, I consider that pastor my friend.

What about someone who won't claim any responsibility for the divide between you? How do you let go and get free in that situation? Well, it's easy to explain it to you, but it was difficult to do. I once had just such a situation. I planned on confronting the person involved. I spent two weeks stewing over it, and preparing to get it off my chest. One day, while on a road trip to preach somewhere, I was talking to the Lord about the situation. He spoke very clearly to me. He instructed me to write down everything I wanted to say when I confronted this person. I thought, "I have no problem doing that. I'm a preacher! I can articulate my position and lay this out like a sermon!"

When I got to the hotel that evening, I sat down and wrote several pages of notes. When I was finished, the Lord spoke to me again. He said, "Now, throw it away and don't ever think about it again." I obeyed the Lord, and I'm glad I did. The Lord knew I needed to get it out, and when I did, I gave it to Him and was immediately free from it. The moral of the story? You are responsible for your heart, not someone else's.

I allowed people to get under my skin. I allowed differences of opinion to get me worked up. I allowed offense to turn into bitterness. I developed callous on top of callous. I wish I had done a better job of guarding my heart. If you will actively guard your heart, you will accelerate the favor of God in your life.

GUARD YOUR HEALTH

Secondly, I would do a better job guarding my health. Pastors believe they're invincible. It's not arrogance. It's the notion that because we are doing the work of the Lord, He will take care of us. The Lord will take care of us, but sometimes what we need is for Him to protect us from ourselves because we neglect and abuse our bodies in the name of ministry. You are no good to anyone if you neglect your health.

There are so many issues I ignored as it relates to my health. When it caught up with me, it was a huge wake-up call. In retrospect, I should have given attention to the following things.

Annual Physicals

I should have been more consistent with my annual physicals and blood work. Had I done so, I could've been taking corrective action. High cholesterol was the only physiological risk factor I had for heart disease. The other two were family history and stress. I should have kept up with my immunizations; pastors don't have time to be sick. Men, especially, hate going to the doctor. I'm no different, but I learned the hard way that making the doc your friend is one of the healthiest habits you can have. Take a multivitamin. It's amazing how something so minor can have such a major impact on how you feel, overall.

Diet

I should have adhered to a healthier diet. When I get to Heaven, I'm going to ask the Lord why all the food we love is so bad for us. Until the last few years, I lived my life eating whatever I wanted. I finally got to where I felt so sluggish, I knew I needed to make some changes to my diet. I did something as simple as limiting sugar and fat intake. I lost almost 40 pounds in a year.

The hardest part for me was limiting sugar. I love sweets. Cake, pie, cookies, cobbler, you name it, I love it. I don't feel like I've had a good meal if I don't have dessert. I also had to learn how to drink coffee without sugar. It was an acquired taste, but I did it. If you put sugar in my coffee now, I'd probably spit it out. Perhaps the most beneficial change was putting a stop to my massive intake of soft drinks and sweet tea, and replacing it with water. (I just heard a pastor down south rebuke me in the name of Jesus.) For you northerners, in the south, sweet tea is believed to be as sacred as anointing oil.

The church culture, to which we are all so accustomed, revolves around food. Everything we do is accompanied by some sort of food. When we go to heaven, one of the first things we're going to do is sit around the table for the marriage supper of the Lamb! Thankfully, we'll have glorified bodies! While on Earth, however, we should watch what we eat. That's difficult when nobody on Earth, and I mean nobody, can cook like church ladies. We've put a lot of chickens into the ministry over the years. When you go to a church dinner, the last thing on your mind is your diet.

I'm a stress eater. Food always makes it better. To quote a movie line, I believe, "Peanut butter fills the cracks of the heart."[10] When I'm stressed, I'm more likely to eat bad and pay the price later. This is a horrible habit and will not make you feel better; it'll only put you into a food coma. It's just a legal form of self-medication.

You don't have to jump on some new diet bandwagon, just eat smart. It's a small course correction that can make a significant difference in the long run.

Exercise

By the time I got serious about physical fitness, the damage was already done; however, I believe it mitigated the severity of my heart disease. Regular exercise is one of those things that must become a priority or you won't make time for it. It must become a habit; it took me several weeks to forge it into my daily routine. Once that happens, you must guard that time because excuses are always abundant.

You don't have to join a gym like I did. You can street jog, mall walk, use a treadmill at home, swim, or ride a bicycle. Just do something to get your body moving and your blood flowing. If you have ever had a workout routine, you know that you always feel better once you are finished, regardless of how bad you feel when you start. There's a sense of accomplishment that comes with a regular routine.

You'll know you've had a good workout routine the next morning when you wake up sore all over. That's a good thing; it means you've activated some muscles that haven't been used much. Don't get discouraged. Take a couple ibuprofen; the soreness will wear off in a couple days. When it does, get back in the gym. Pain is the indicator you're doing something right. My Lord, that'll preach!

In my experience, an average workout routine should be accompanied by extra protein in your diet. It helps the soreness and assists in muscle rebuilding. I use protein shakes after workouts. I'll admit, physical fitness can become an obsession, but I consider it a good obsession with healthy results.

The bottom line is that you get some exercise, whatever that looks like for you. You will feel better, have more energy, and may even lose a few pounds in the process.

Sleep

I should have given more attention to sleep patterns, and prioritized my rest. I have always been a night owl. I feel more productive at night. Many nights I would fall asleep in my recliner and then migrate to the bed; I very seldom slept enough. It took a toll on my health.

I've learned to manage my sleep patterns now. This is another area your doctor can help you with. If you're having trouble sleeping, there's nothing wrong with taking something to help you sleep. Melatonin is natural, over the counter, and effective. If you require extra care, your doc can prescribe you something to help. I used to be one of those persons who refused to take anything for any reason. As I have gotten older, I've learned that I was just being stubborn and could possibly benefit from the help. I don't take something daily to sleep, only when I'm struggling to get the rest I need. I've found that once I get in a good sleep rhythm, I have no trouble at all.

I'm certainly not a medical professional, but I know first hand the impact physical health can have on your ministry. You don't have to take my advice. I've just shared some practical things that have worked for me. Do what works for you, but don't ignore your health. It matters.

GUARD YOUR HEAD

Thirdly, I would do a better job guarding my head. Perhaps, the toughest battle we fight is between our ears. The battle of the mind is no joke. This is one of the things that affected my sleep so severely. I would lay down at night but couldn't shut off my mind. I would lay there and be tormented by everything I hadn't accomplished. I would agonize over my mistakes, shortcomings, inferiorities and the like. I was powerless to stop it.

I know 2 Corinthians 10:5 says, "We demolish arguments and every pretension that sets itself up against the knowledge of God, and we take captive every thought to make it obedient to Christ."

And, I know Isaiah 26:3 says, "You keep him in perfect peace whose mind is stayed on you because he trusts in you."

I've been a student of scripture since I was an adolescent; I know what the Word says. Sometimes knowing the Scripture and putting it into practice can be totally different things. I needed to be a better gate-keeper of the people and the information I let into my head.

Not everyone who has an opinion is worthy of claiming a piece of your brain. You can't afford to allow just anyone to speak into your life. Guarding your mind is about choosing wisdom and rejecting foolishness.

"Fools find no pleasure in understanding but delight in airing their own opinions." Proverbs 18:2

Too often, I allowed people to get into my head with their foolishness. For me, this had roots in my need for affirmation. I wanted everyone to like me. When I felt someone was at odds with me, it would pervade my thoughts and I would agonize for days before I could get it out of my head. It was an exhausting process. I have always envied people who never seem to be affected by negative words and opinions.

I'm in a different place today. I don't struggle with this as I used to. I don't wrestle with others' opinions. I have peace in my mind. I sleep well. What's different? Firstly, I'm not pastoring, anymore. Secondly, my stress level is much lower. Thirdly, I have learned how to give things to the Lord, and let Him worry about it.

"In peace I will lie down and sleep, for you alone, Lord, make me dwell in safety." Psalm 4:8

"I lie down and sleep; I wake again because the Lord sustains me." Psalm 3:5

GUARD YOUR HOME

Finally, I would do a better job guarding my home. I don't mean my house. I mean my home. Guarding your home means guarding your family and personal time. Effective time management is a skill. You either have it or you must learn it. The alternative is chaos. Time is like money. Let's say you budget $150 per week for groceries and $50 per week for gas. If you spend $175 on groceries, you have to take money from your gas budget or another category to cover your overspending. Budgeting time works the same way. With time management, the category that always gets used to cover overspending is personal time. The more you spend elsewhere, the less personal time you have.

When you set your home budget, you have to prioritize categories. What categories are the most important that you would never borrow from? Your mortgage category? Insurance? Car notes? You would never think of using the mortgage money on something else, it's too important! You must prioritize time in the same way. When prioritizing time categories, I would assume you would consider work to be most important. If you don't show up, you don't get paid, and perhaps can't keep your job. Next, you have family time, kid's activities, worship and other church obligations, and the list grows from there. The last thing on most people's list is personal time. When that is least important, it will always get used to make up for overspending in other categories.

Your home should be your sanctuary. It's the place where you should be free from the noise and stress of the world, and the ministry. At home is where you should be able to take all your hats off and just be you; safe from judgement, stereotypes, and criticism. If you don't have peace in your home, you don't have peace anywhere.

When a pastor allows the stress of ministry to breach his home, it can affect his relationships with his family. I know this first hand. A bad day in the office usually followed me home. The last thing I wanted was for my children to resent the church because of the way a difficult pastorate directly affected them. Thankfully, I was successful enough in shielding them from the stress that they both went on to be involved in local church ministry.

Guarding your home is also about having unity. If you don't have it, your home life can be difficult. What amuses me is, people come to church on Sunday morning angry, after fighting with kids, fighting with their spouse, fighting with traffic, etc., thinking the pastor's family is any different. Many Sundays, I would arrive at the church, wanting to do nothing more than get to my office without being detected. I wanted to have a clear heart and head when I stepped in the pulpit, and felt I needed to isolate myself to preserve clarity.

Pastor's must work hard to guard their homes, just like anyone else. In my experience, if the enemy can get me in the wrong frame of mind before I even get out of my house, it can affect the whole church that day.

Unity in the home is the best defense against stress and strife. If you don't have it and don't know how to get it, I would suggest getting into family counseling. If you're too proud to take your family to counseling, you're not ready to receive what I'm saying.

The Lord has a way of allowing your pride to be destroyed if you won't swallow it willingly.

There's nothing more important than guarding your home. When you are no longer a pastor, you will still be a spouse and parent. You belong to your family before you ever belong to a congregation.

HIND SIGHT

Change is difficult. But, wouldn't you rather make a few small course corrections now than to be way off course later? Take these suggestions for what they are, just suggestions.

In addition to taking my own personal inventory, I would have solicited the input of a heavy lifter. A spotter who can teach me how to reach my goals and fulfill my destiny.

The question is, would I have listened? I don't know the answer. Think about this. The phrase, "Hind sight is 20/20" is inaccurate. 20/20 means I can see at twenty feet what a person should normally see at twenty feet.[11] I should be able to see 20/20 looking forward. If I can't, I have a vision problem. Hind sight should be much clearer than 20/20. When you look back, you have the advantage of putting things under a microscope and examining closely what you see. Perhaps, if I had 20/20 forward vision, I would have understood the value of allowing someone who's been where I am to speak into my life with hind sight, or a microscopic view.

Find you a mentor with some battle scars. Glean from the wisdom they've taken from their battlefield. If they've examined their struggle, in hind sight, with a microscopic view, perhaps they can superimpose that view over your current situation and impart some wisdom into your life.

"Though one may be overpowered, two can defend themselves.
A cord of three strands is not quickly broken." Ecclesiastes 4:12

"Lord, how many are my foes! How many rise up against me! Many are saying of me, 'God will not deliver him.' But you, Lord, are a shield around me, my glory, the One who lifts my head high."

(Psalm 3:1-3)

CHAPTER NINE

The Breakdown

Remember, from page one we agreed we need Jesus in the center of our brokenness to put the pieces back together. Again, my goal here is not to spiritualize the struggle, it is to be transparent and real about what goes on inside a broken pastor. As much as I'd like you to believe I was so spiritual that I floated above the surface of the ground and was untouchable by the world, it just wasn't true. Not for me. Not for anyone. This book is about taking off the mask and showing you the human behind the pulpit. Even at that, I'm not even scratching the surface. Working on this project invoked so many very real and heavy emotions as I relived some tough moments, but I have done so in hopes that recounting these things will somehow speak life into your barrenness.

Burnout doesn't come at you all at once; it creeps in slowly in stages. Based on my own experience, I want to share with you seven stages to watch for.

1. Disillusionment

2. The need for affirmation

3. Resistance

4. Estrangement

5. Disorientation

6. Resentment

7. Detachment

I want to point out that the early stages of burnout mirror the early stages of a successful ministry. Every pastor goes through disillusionment, the need for affirmation and resistance; they are normal in the relationship formed between a pastor and congregation. At a critical time in a pastor's journey, however, a crossroad will come which distinguishes between the path to success and the path to burnout. I am not saying burnout is necessarily a choice; I'm saying there are internal and external factors that can create a detour in the road. Internal factors can include spiritual maturity, character, integrity, and physical, mental and emotional health. The external factors include family life, support system, people, relationship with ecclesiastical authority, etc. A pastor's reactions and responses to those factors will, ultimately, affect the outcome.

If burnout is allowed to run its course unchecked, it will inevitably lead to a pastor quitting, being in physical and/or mental distress, having a moral failure, or any combination. This is a raw look at my battle so you will be able to identify and get help before it goes too far. If it has already gone too far, you're not without hope. God is a restorer and He wants to give you a resurgence!

THE LAW OF AVERAGE

The progression of pastoral burnout is summed up in what I call the *Law of Average.* This is not to be confused with the law of averages, which is the belief that a certain outcome is inevitable because it is statistically possible. What I'm talking about is the slow, gradual corrosion of a pastor's ministry.

The simple definition of "average" is adding several quantities and dividing by the number of quantities. The term originates from the practice of mitigating liability from goods lost or damaged at sea in the late fifteenth century. The French word from which it evolved, *avarie*, means "damage to ship or cargo." Simply, when goods being shipped by sea were lost or damaged because of a storm or other catastrophe, the owner of the goods and the owner of the ship would share the loss so neither were held liable for the complete loss. They split the difference, or average. The word "average" literally means damaged goods.[12]

As a pastor, I came to the place where I felt like damaged goods; not worthy of success, not worthy of promotion, not worthy of respect and certainly not worthy of the anointing and blessings of God. In that season of my life, I resigned myself to the belief that all I would ever be is average, and it almost killed me. I gave up my visions of being used greatly by the Lord. Burnout begins by deciding "average" is good enough. It's the most dangerous place for a pastor to be, because what is average seeks to eliminate what is excellent. This is what I refer to as the *Law of Average.*

DISILLUSIONMENT

Every pastor experiences disillusionment. It comes when the honeymoon is over and the first sign of reality sets in. After the revelation of our calling, we emerge from seminary with a keen sense of altruism in our minds, a passion in our hearts and a light in our eyes. We set out to do ministry with a sense that we are blessed and honored to walk in the calling and a belief that we are going to make a difference. As time passes, we retain the honor of the calling, but we can slowly become jaded by the realization ministry is nothing like we were taught it would be.

I'll never forget the day my pastoral honeymoon ended. It was a warm summer evening during the county fair. I had received a call earlier in the day from one of the church board members. This brother informed me he and some of the other board members wanted a meeting to discuss my performance. To this day, I have no idea what they were upset about. I was 26 years old and doing the best I knew how to do. I gave them my best sermons on Sunday, visited the hospitals, loved people, carried out my administrative tasks and whatever else fell in my lap. I didn't know what I had done and was hurt that anyone had a problem with me. I felt like I had been falsely accused of some crime and I was getting ready to step into the courtroom to be put on trial. It was horrible.

My parents raised me, not only to love the Lord, but to love the pastor. I never once heard my parents say a cross word about our pastor. In fact, the pastor and his family were frequent guests in our home. I grew up with a profound respect for the ministry. Maybe that's why it hit me so hard when people, to whom I was trying to minister, got sideways with me. I felt like I had been punched in the stomach and had the wind knocked out of me. This isn't how this was supposed to happen. I didn't know how to reconcile this. This is the rest of the story about my betrayal experience.

I'm pleased to report, the Lord rescued me. Before I walked across the parking lot from the parsonage to the church, I prayed once more for direction. The Lord spoke and, ultimately, taught me a valuable lesson. He instructed me to throw a towel over my shoulder and carry a basin of water with me when I walked into the church office. He said, "Tell the men that have assembled; before the meeting begins you are going to wash their feet." So, that's what I did.

When I walked through the door they were waiting for me. I did exactly as I was instructed. When I told them what I intended to do, one of the board members spoke up and said, "Pastor, before you wash my feet, I'm going to wash your feet." That was it. Whatever the matter of contention had been, it immediately dissipated as every man there followed suit, lined up at my desk and, one by one, washed my feet. When they were finished, I obeyed the Lord, going around the room, washing their feet and praying over them. Before we walked out of that room we were hugging necks, asking for forgiveness, crying and loving on one another. To this day, I don't know what they had been upset about.

Although God honored my acts of obedience and humility, brought unity to my church board, and taught me a valuable lesson on managing conflict, I was never the same again. I knew the honeymoon was over. I was thankful God had rescued me from the clutches of people, and I knew I would need Him to help me navigate those new waters from that day forward.

THE NEED FOR AFFIRMATION

It's natural to seek affirmation. I seem to need it more than most and I despise that about myself. It has often caused me to look to the wrong people and places for approval. My experience with disillusionment led me to seek the affirmation of people to avoid living that awful experience again. That's dangerous. It got Saul into trouble in 1 Samuel 15:24. "Then Saul said to Samuel, "I have sinned. I violated the LORD's command and your instructions. I was afraid of the men and so I gave in to them."

The Lord commanded Saul, through Samuel, to completely destroy the Amalekites. They were to leave nothing alive and bring back nothing. The Lord wanted them annihilated. However, Saul disobeyed the Lord and brought back some of the valuable things such as the best of the sheep, cattle, fat calves, and lambs. Everything that was good. Verse 9 says they were "unwilling" to destroy these things. Bad move. Saul looked to the people for approval (at least he blamed it on them) and it cost him the throne.

Now listen, it's perfectly healthy and good practice for a leader to get buy-in from the people they lead. Buy-in leads to a sense of ownership and dedication to a given endeavor. Whenever I went into a church board meeting with a new project, I had already been planting the seeds for the idea. By the time I presented the project in a meeting, I had buy-in. I always said the best way to get something done in a board meeting was to present it in such a way they thought it was their idea. There is a difference, however, between healthy buy-in and unhealthy affirmation seeking.

Inevitably, there always seemed to be that one person or family in the church to which I looked to see if they approved with what I said or did. If I had their nod, and therefore their support, I knew I'd be okay. If I didn't, I lost sleep over it and agonized over every word, look, phone call, text, attitude, etc., reading into things and beating myself up. It drove me absolutely crazy.

In my law enforcement capacity, I have testified in court countless times. One day I was on the stand as the arresting officer in a DUI case. The prosecutor, a fairly new attorney, was questioning me to establish the state's case. Very quickly I picked up on a pattern. Each time he asked me a question and I answered, he would glance over at the judge. After a while it began to bug me because I could only think of two reasons for that. Either he wasn't confident in his ability or he wasn't as confident in my answers as I was.

I realized my pattern of looking to certain people for affirmation was evidence of my lack of confidence in myself. Those people recognized that and often exploited it for their benefit. People are smart. They will pick up on it when you always seek affirmation and approval from the same people. I believe it also frustrates people, because they don't know if you lack confidence in yourself or it's your confidence in them that is wavering.

What I discovered is, there will always come an intersection in the road where you will obey the direction of the Lord and the decision will directly contradict the will of the people whose affirmation you've always sought. The result is a falling out. If you've ever served as a pastor you've experienced a falling out with someone you once considered an ally. The hard truth is the people who meet you at the airport when you arrive will almost always be the people who rise against you when the going gets rough.

My need for affirmation was part of my downfall. I'm a pretty sensitive guy; I don't like it when people are upset at me. Thus, the reason I sought affirmation from people. What a contradiction it seems to have a pastor's heart but still have to maintain thick skin. You must have both to stay alive in this game.

What's the solution? A friend once told me I have reckless obedience (this is where I got the term). He defined it as the resolve to obey the word of the Lord regardless of the fallout. Look, we all have the need for a certain level of affirmation, but you must be able to make the unpopular decisions, knowing not everyone will approve, when you've heard from the Lord.

Here's an example of reckless obedience which, quite frankly, made me extremely nervous. In 2007 a missionary came to my church to promote his project. He shared the story of Pastor Paco from Reynosa, Mexico, who had a congregation of about three hundred people but no building to worship in. During that presentation, the Lord spoke to me. I wasn't sure how it would play out when I stood up at the end of that service to inform the congregation we were going to build a church in Reynosa. We hadn't held a board meeting. I didn't take a poll. I just obeyed the Lord. That day we raised, in offerings and pledges, approximately $10,000. I sure was glad the Lord came through that day. I was praying like David in Psalm 31, "In you, O Lord, do I take refuge; let me never be put to shame; in your righteousness deliver me!"

Before it was over with, another church in the area partnered with us and together we built a church in Reynosa, Mexico. Were there dissenters? Oh, yes. Did I get resistance? Yes. Did it matter? No. Now, when I see a live video feed of Centro Cristiano Victoria, I am reminded I've never been sorry for having reckless obedience.

RESISTANCE

I am not suggesting resistance is abnormal. In fact, I don't know of a pastor anywhere that hasn't had resistance to their ministry. I'll go a step further and submit I can't find anyone in scripture, who God greatly used, that didn't have resistance to their ministry. Resistance is normal. How you react to resistance is the crossroad that can determine your future.

When you are a person who has an unhealthy need for affirmation, you tend to not handle resistance well. It's easy for you to take things personally. If you don't keep this issue in balance, you begin to consider every opposing view as an indictment against your character and leadership, when it's just an opposing view.

I'll confess, I had a hard time dealing with resistance as a pastor. As difficult as it can be, it's necessary. In the gym, resistance is what builds muscle. The more resistance you can handle, the stronger you become. The stronger you become, the more resistance you can handle. The same principle applies to ministry.

I know people who are masters at handling resistance and conflict management. They thrive on it. They don't get upset, rattled or even nervous when they encounter a problem. I'm not one of those people. When I was a state director, I worked with an overseer who had the gift. When a situation would arise, he would develop a strategy and say something like, "Okay, Jeff, this is what we're going to do." I believe he loved the challenge. I have always respected him for the way he navigated and resolved issues effectively.

Resistance can be a sign you're going in the right direction. I read a quote by Perry Stone recently in which he said, "The anointing attracts attacks."[13] When you carry the oil on your life, you are already a target of the enemy. A by-product of spiritual warfare is spiritual attack. It's like "the list" I wrote about earlier. If you're on that list,

Satan wishes to get your name blotted off the list. The old timers used to put it this way, "When the Lord starts blessing, the devil starts messing." I always knew when I was onto something, because the resistance of the enemy would become heated. Sometimes the enemy's resistance came through people.

My reaction to resistance, over time, contributed to my burnout. I wish I could tell you I was good at handling the pressure like that overseer, but at times I allowed it to get to me. When people resisted, I often spent hours obsessing over it. Why would anyone be against someone who was working so hard to minister to people? Why would anyone pose resistance to the building of the church and the kingdom? For me, resistance translated to rejection. I let it eat away at my confidence. I let it affect my mood. I let it push me toward isolation. I let it corrode my passion. Eventually, I let it rob me of my joy.

When I was just starting out in the gym, I was giving so much attention to the weight that I lost the importance of good form. Instead of allowing the resistance of the weight to make me stronger, I was plateauing and setting myself up for injury. I made the correction in the gym, but it didn't occur to me I needed to make the correction in ministry. Instead of allowing the resistance to make me stronger, I let it break me down.

This is where I took the wrong turn at the crossroad and started heading for burnout.

ESTRANGEMENT

Estrangement in ministry happens when you lose the closeness you once had with key people around you. A pastor always has an inner circle, people who are faithful, committed and heavily involved in the operations of the church. This is truer the larger the congregation. When a church grows, a pastor's ability to be one-on-one with the membership decreases. That pastor will often have to shift their paradigm to begin pastoring leaders so the leaders can pastor the people. In contrast, there are others that are always on the fringe. You will likely see them about two out of four Sundays a month however, they're not connected to the ministries of the church. They come late, leave early and sometimes intentionally avoid contact. They don't want to be locked in to extracurricular commitments, they just want to attend church periodically. Pastors do not normally have significant interaction with fringe folks because they just aren't around.

By virtue of opportunity, pastors forge strong relationships with the people in their circle. They have them as guests in their home, marry them, dedicate their children to the Lord, burry their parents, visit their loved ones in the hospital, and pour themselves into them with no expectation of anything in return. When someone in the pastor's inner circle suddenly turns on them, it causes serious pain (There's the betrayal factor again). It leaves a pastor second guessing himself and racking his brain, trying to figure out where he went wrong. It's more impactful than someone on the fringe leaving the church; it's personal. It's almost like losing a family member; the pastor becomes the estranged family member.

The magic question is, why would someone in a pastor's inner circle turn against them? It can be related to a pastor making an unpopular decision. Something I learned the hard way was, never underestimate someone's loyalty to someone else.

Several years ago, I was forced to make a tough staff decision. I terminated someone who was widely loved by the congregation and had been an employee of the church five years longer than I had been there. When I say I was forced, that's exactly what happened. I was forced to make a cut. The only decision I had the discretion to make was who to terminate. I was going to be the bad guy no matter what I did. It was an impossible situation. I made the decision to terminate the person I felt would leave the smallest void in the ministry of the church at the time. Thus, I lost the support and loyalty of one of the most influential families in the church. I underestimated their loyalty to the terminated employee. I became estranged from the family. They eventually left the church, but not before they could cause some sticky situations. It was painful.

Estrangement creates ancillary problems. This is why I have an issue with one family or group within a congregation having too much responsibility. When you depend upon someone so heavily to get things done, you are one unpopular decision away from being a one-man show. When the pastor becomes estranged from an influential family, he is often left holding the bag and blamed for the fallout. The pastor is forced to do damage control, which distracts them from focusing on more pressing responsibilities.

I'll also confess, it's hard to leave this kind of stuff at the office. You take it home with you. You lose sleep over it. It consumes your thoughts and overshadows everything else you have on your mind.

When I started ministry way back when, I wanted to preach the gospel, win people to Jesus, and make a difference in the world. I didn't sign up for this kind of abuse. I didn't handle the resistance well, I became estranged from people I thought were fiercely loyal, and I eventually became very disoriented.

DISORIENTATION

Disorientation is a loss of your sense of direction, position, or relationship with your surroundings. Spatial disorientation, sometimes experienced by pilots or divers, happens when you lose your physical reference point and your sensory input begins to conflict with reality. A pilot experiencing spatial disorientation has lost sight of the horizon and may think he's flying level when he's banking. This was said to be the cause of JFK Jr.'s plane crash in Martha's Vineyard in 1999.[14] When a diver experiences spatial disorientation, he is usually diving in deep water with little to no visibility. The pressure causes a temporary impairment of senses resulting in the diver losing his sense of direction to the surface. These are both dangerous situations.

A pastor can also experience disorientation when ministering in an extreme environment. When a pastor loses sight of the horizon, he begins to fly blind and is in danger of a tail spin. When a pastor is under an enormous amount of pressure (like the diver in 200 feet of water), the feeling of being "in too deep" or "in over your head" can set in making it hard to navigate back to the surface, leaving the pastor to drown.

Pastoral disorientation isn't something that happens overnight. It's a gradual loss of direction, triggered by a prolonged exposure to extreme circumstances. When a pastor has no peace from the noise, it can become overwhelming and overbearing.

Disorientation is the stage where people begin to notice the difference in a pastor's public presence. We are normally good at hiding our feelings and putting our best face forward, but when you get disoriented you begin to lose your ability to hide your fear. A couple of years ago, my wife and I were in the Caribbean on one of the U.S. Virgin Islands. We decided to go snorkeling. I've been snorkeling before; it's not difficult and really no big deal. But on this particular occasion, I got too deep and water came down my snorkel tube just as I was taking a breath. The feeling of sucking water down into my lungs sent me into instant panic. For a moment, I experienced a mild form of spatial disorientation and I lost my sense of direction to the surface. It didn't take me long to get my bearings and get my head above water, but it seemed like an eternity when I desperately needed air. My wife could tell there was something wrong. As I popped up out of the water, gasping for air and coughing violently, she made her way over to me to make sure I was okay. It was kind of embarrassing.

That encounter with sea water resembled the feeling of pastoral disorientation I experienced. I felt like I was in too deep, gasping for air, and almost in a panic. I lost my bearings. I didn't trust my relationships, I didn't trust my abilities, I didn't trust people, and I certainly didn't trust the process. I lost my sense of direction. I didn't know what to do or where to go. I was desperately looking for the surface but couldn't tell which way it was.

It's important to note at this point, my disillusionment and response to resistance grew significantly worse. My need for affirmation turned into a regrouping of my allies, and a re-evaluation of my inner circle. This is probably where I began to slowly isolate myself.

I have always been goal and vision driven. I believe in strong mission and vision statements. I believe in casting vision and leading people toward accomplishing the vision. I held "Vision" banquets every year to celebrate the accomplishments of the past and refocus the congregation on the future. The prolonged struggle I endured, however, began to affect my sense of vision.

What resulted was a tunnel vision effect. My gaze shifted downward. My focus narrowed. In essence, I began to hang my head. My goals were reduced to just trying to make it through the day. This is survival mode. When survival mode ensued, I couldn't function beyond what I needed to do to get through the present. I began having trouble planning or thinking about anything that was in the future more than two weeks. When I sucked down that sea water and began struggling to get to the surface, I wasn't thinking about what I would have for dinner that evening, or what an enjoyable vacation I was having. The only thing I cared about was getting air. Me, the guy with O.C.D. who planned the sermon series calendar a year in advance. I was so disoriented, so consumed with surviving another day that my ability to plan into the future was almost non-existent.

Disorientation causes you to lose your sense of relationship to the people around you. You begin to confuse allies with dissenters. You begin to misjudge the intentions of the people closest to you who are genuinely standing with you. Like a soldier on the battlefield who has a hard time distinguishing the friendly from the foe, I began having trouble identifying my allies. Going through this is absolutely horrible; it's the loneliest feeling I've ever had in my life. How is it possible to experience such a deep sense of loneliness when you're surrounded by people? When your struggle is private, the outward manifestations of fear, frustration and anger that people begin to see are confusing to them because they don't know the underlying reason. We all know how easily people get offended. A misunderstood word, look, response, etc., out of fear, frustration or anger could cost you influence.

Disorientation is when you realize you're no longer in control. Now, if there is one thing pastors all have in common (besides the obvious) it's that we all have type A personalities. We like to be in control. If you don't believe me, try preaching to a room full of preachers. I've had the privilege of preaching in a few state camp meetings over the years and I can tell you, preaching to preachers is intimidating. When preachers hear preachers preach, we are preaching it differently in our heads. It's just what we do. We are expected to be dominant personalities and we either have the gift or must work at it; the latter was certainly the case for me. Feeling like you're losing control causes panic and insecurity in a pastor. If disorientation is not dealt with it may lead to inevitable crash and burn.

RESENTMENT

By the time a pastor reaches the resentment stage, serious damage has been done. Body, mind, soul and spirit are affected in this process. Resentment is rooted in feeling angered, annoyed, and hurt provoked by what is perceived as unfair treatment. I felt unfairly treated by people, unfairly treated by superiors, unfairly treated by the system, and I felt a lot of resentment toward certain people.

I thought, "If I had been dealt a better hand, things wouldn't have become so bad. If the overseer had moved me when I asked, I wouldn't be here in this mess. If I had just been presented with the right opportunity, I would be in a different place." I didn't resent the Lord, but I began to feel like I didn't deserve anything better. Had I been a better pastor, maybe He would have given me a better opportunity. Had I prayed more, or worked harder, perhaps I would have been worth more. You and I both know, that kind of condemnation doesn't come from the Lord, but I was in such a weak, worn out, and vulnerable place in my life, I didn't have any fight left in me.

I never lost my belief in the Word of God, nor did I ever reach a place where I stopped believing the Lord could move on my behalf. I just came to a place where I believed I wasn't deserving of His intervention and perhaps He wasn't willing to clean up the mess I felt I had made. I even resented myself.

Resentment is a dangerous place. Resentment is often about placing blame. I can only resent you if I blame you in some way for my pain. If I blame you, I can't be well until I forgive you, and I can't forgive you if I resent you. It's a fatal cycle. Resentment is the chain that has to be broken for real freedom to take place.

Resentment can only be broken by allowing the Lord to change your heart. I'm thankful God performed a miracle in my life and broke the spirit of resentment that had settled in my heart. I'll share more of that story later.

DETACHMENT

Detachment is the last stage of the burnout process I went through. This is where it all ended and I broke down. For me, detachment was a defense mechanism to prevent further pain. I began to relate pain and conflict to certain people and places and I began avoiding them. I began to slowly release my emotional attachments. For instance, I stopped going to my office unless it was necessary. That place had become a trigger for me. I had too many difficult meetings there. I had too many painful conversations there. There had been confrontations there. Being in the room just triggered too many emotions. Consequently, I would call my administrative assistant and tell her I was working from home that day and to call or text me if she needed anything so I could avoid the office.

I avoided people, and not just the toxic people. I started avoiding the people that never gave me any trouble. Why? Because I knew they were talkers and would stop in the office just to visit. I knew they were happy people and would expect me to be as well. I knew they would take thirty to forty-five minutes of my day, just talking. They weren't difficult people; they were my supporters. I just didn't have it in me. I wanted to be alone. I was beginning to emotionally detach. I was walling myself off from the world around me, building an emotional cocoon in which I would be safer.

My detachment wasn't limited to my staff and congregation; I began to isolate myself from family as well. My parents, sister and brother-in-law and extended family all lived hours away, so we communicated by phone regularly. We've always been a close family, but in my distress, I even began to close them out. It wasn't because they had somehow contributed to my pain, but because I wanted to protect them from what I felt I had become.

Detachment was as much about shielding people from me as it was about shielding myself from people. I didn't know who I was anymore. My self-esteem and confidence were practically non-existent. I was afraid of what I would say to people and how I would present myself. Regardless of my severe burnout, I was still somehow trying to keep the ship afloat. I was still preaching my heart out every Sunday, because that's the one thing I never lost my love for. Nothing has ever made me feel more fulfilled and complete than getting on stage behind a pulpit and declaring the Word of the Lord. It's what I've lived for since I was fifteen years old. I'm thankful the Lord still used me despite myself and the bad place I was in at the time.

Toward the end, I stopped going to the office altogether. I stopped having weekly staff meetings. I stopped returning phone calls. I deferred hospital visits to elders. I was almost completely detached. So detached that one day in a face-to-face conversation with my overseer, I heard myself say, "If the church burned down tomorrow, it wouldn't make any difference to me." I'm ashamed to share that with you; I do so to illustrate how broken and wounded I had become. Of course, that was my pain talking, not what was in my heart.

In September of 2013 I asked for and was granted an emergency three-month sabbatical. Unfortunately, it was too little too late for me. About six weeks into the sabbatical I had my heart attack. I never returned to the pastorate. I stepped to the pulpit one last time on the first Sunday of 2014 to resign.

After my resignation, I completely broke down. My body had already failed. I crashed emotionally, mentally and spiritually. I went through a moral failure, a subsequent divorce, and severe depression. Apparently, this was it. My name had been taken off the list. I would never be greatly used of God. The vision I had at sixteen years old, of preaching to thousands of people, would never become reality. I had been inoculated with failure. I was done.

"Brothers and sisters, if someone is caught in a sin, you who live by the Spirit should restore that person gently. But watch yourselves, or you also may be tempted."

⊢···⊣

(Ephesians 6:1)

CHAPTER TEN

The Golden Hour

The breakdown was avoidable. The responsibility for my failures lies squarely on me. He who blames his actions on someone else is a fool. That's from Second Opinions chapter one, Wolf's Unauthorized Translation (WUT).

Having said that, if I had received treatment for my symptoms, perhaps I could've avoided a complete breakdown. When a soldier is wounded on the battlefield, whether it's enemy fire, friendly fire, or self-inflicted, his survival will largely depend on the rescue effort. If he is bandaged up, his bleeding is stopped, and he's medevac'd to safety, he has a higher chance of survival.

I was privileged to be affiliated with one of the world's foremost Full Gospel organizations for more than two decades. During my tenure, I was honored with great opportunities for ministry. I will always be thankful for the experiences and Kingdom connections

I have had as a result of that covering. Unfortunately, in the height of my burnout experience, the organization was not prepared to intervene on my behalf. It wasn't until my struggle became public that my bleeding was taken seriously.

I needed help long before I threw in the towel. When I sought help, it seemed inaccessible. I sincerely believe they didn't know how to help me. If my wounds had been bound up, perhaps I could've made a complete recovery and been put back on the front line. Please hear my heart; I'm not blaming an organization for my actions or inactions. I'm simply saying, organizations have a responsibility to stand with their pastors. The church had piloted a few mentoring and support programs in the years leading up to my burnout, many of which I participated in. Regardless, something was missing. The subject of burnout hasn't really been mentioned above a whisper until recently.

Someone asked me, "What could the organization have done differently to help you?" Well, imagine you've just been shot. You're on the ground bleeding, your very life draining from you, and you're paralyzed from shock. When you call 911 (from the phone already in your hand) and tell them you're dying, they ask for your mailing address and assure you they will mail you directions to the hospital. Pause and let that sink in. That is the most realistic analogy I can imagine to describe the ineptness of the system to help wounded pastors in time to save them.

The system is broken and desperately needs to be fixed. We need a revolution of healing and restoration in the church from the top down. I'm not the kind of person to point out a problem without contributing to the solution. I don't have all the answers, but I know what I needed. I needed someone to come to me, instead of requiring me to make all the effort. If I could get to the hospital on my own, I wouldn't be laying here on the ground!

When you are seriously injured and call 911, you need the person on the other end of the phone to send you an ambulance as quickly as possible. Lights and sirens! It's an emergency. When they get there, you need them to bring their tools and equipment to where you are lying. You need them to reassure you they're going to take care of you and everything's going to be okay. You need them to put an oxygen mask on your face, an I.V. in your arm and start giving you the oxygen and fluids you need to help stabilize your condition. You need them to cut away your layers to expose your wound so the bleeding can be stopped. You need them to lift you off the ground, onto the cot, and into the back of the ambulance. Then you need them to drive you to the hospital. On the way, you need them to continue to monitor your vital signs and talk you through your pain. The church should take a page from the emergency medical playbook.

I've watched EMTs work. They're very good at their jobs. I've seen them extract people from impossible situations. I've watched them perform life saving measures for a solid thirty minutes when they couldn't get someone's heart to beat, but refused to give up. I've seen them show compassion and empathy for people who were less than gracious. I've been there when they saved someone's life.

Not only have I watched them work, I've been their patient. If only the church had cared for me like the medics did on November 13, 2013. I needed the denominational red tape to be removed so the rescuers could come to me, because I didn't have the strength to go to them. They gave me directions to the hospital, but I didn't have any fuel in my tank.

PRESSING THE PANIC BUTTON

The organizational system I was in dealt with bleeding shepherds mostly in a reactive manner. There was a restoration program, but its focus was mainly disciplinary; it was a program to help pastors who had already fallen. It began with surrendering your credentials, and receiving instructions in the mail about how to set up counseling at headquarters, which happens to be 350 miles away from my home. It was anemic, at best.

There was no real effort to address the problem of burnout and its effects, when the intervention could've made a difference. Help was only offered after I was already burned out, and my struggle had become public. It was way too late, then.

A bleeding shepherd should be able to press the panic button! He should be able to rest assured that when he does so, help is coming!

I believe more pastors would press the panic button if they knew they could safely do so. If the stigma is removed from burnout and failure, I believe they will reach out. No one is going to reveal their wounds if they believe it will jeopardize their livelihood, and their position will be yanked out from under them. They need to feel safe, stable, and secure.

When I suffered the heart attack in 2013, the doctors told me I'd be off work for two months. My Chief of Police didn't send me a letter outlining the reasons I was now unfit for duty. I wasn't suspended or penalized; I was uplifted. My brothers and sisters in blue showed up at the hospital, sent cards and messages, called my phone, and were there for me. My coworkers picked up my case load. When I ran out of sick time before the doctor released me for full duty, they came together and donated sick time so I wouldn't go without a paycheck until I was well. The church should sing off the same song sheet as the police community.

I would have died that day if I had refused treatment for fear of losing my job and livelihood. I didn't have to, though. I knew the resources were available to keep me until I recovered. Bleeding shepherds are dying for fear that showing their wounds will put their families in jeopardy.

Here's another nugget from the police community. When an officer is involved in a shooting, a supervisor will come to the scene to take charge. Eventually, the supervisor will need to take the officer's gun; it is now evidence. The officer will be sent to the hospital for any injuries or medical issues, and will be placed on paid administrative leave while the incident is being investigated. This is all standard operating procedure for most law enforcement agencies in the country.

When I went to supervisor school, I learned a valuable lesson from a sergeant who had managed an officer involved shooting scene. He said that when it came time to take the officer's gun, the sergeant gave the officer his gun. This is important. This officer has just been involved in a stressful critical incident. Taking his gun could send the wrong message that he has done something wrong (assuming his actions are justified). It could also leave him feeling unsafe and unable to protect himself (which is especially damaging if he has just been shot at). When the sergeant gave him his own gun, it was a gesture to assure him he was going to be okay.

Back to bleeding shepherds. Do I believe in correction when there has been a moral failure? Yes. Do I believe restoration sometimes requires a pastor to step away from public life for a season? Yes. He can't get well otherwise. Do I believe the process should be

129

punitive rather than reconstructive? No. Do I believe the process should cause further emotional, mental, and financial distress to the pastor? No.

True correction brings affection. When I was growing up, my dad had a leather ministry. When I got out of line, he ministered to me. That ministry changed my life. It taught me how to behave. What I respect about my dad is that he would always tell me why I was being punished, and after the correction, he would take me in his arms and tell me he loved me. Correction was always followed by affection.

I believe the church has been so focused on dealing with violations of ecclesiastical bylaws and practical commitments, it overshadows the sense of compassion and purpose for restoring someone who has fallen. Ecclesiastical correction should never take precedence over saving bleeding shepherds. Our priorities should reflect the urgency of restoring a life and ministry. Time is of the essence. A pastor's life could depend on how the church responds. Treatment has to precede diagnosis. If a patient bleeds out for lack of treatment, the diagnosis won't matter.

THE GOLDEN HOUR

The Golden Hour is a medical term that refers to the period of time, following a traumatic injury, in which a patient's chance of survival increases if proper treatment is obtained.

This term was coined by Dr. R. Adams Cowley, known as the father of trauma medicine and the founder of the United States' first trauma center at the University of Maryland in 1958.[15] He stated, "There is a golden hour between life and death. If you are critically injured, you have less than 60 minutes to survive. You might not die right then; it may be three days or two weeks later — but something has happened in your body that is irreparable."[16] This doctrine is the basis for modern medical trauma teams.

Dr. Cowley began his long and distinguished medical career as a combat surgeon in post-World War II Europe in 1946.[17] Because of his research and influence, the Golden Hour rule is used in combat medicine to this day.

Dr. Cowley explained, "If I can get to you... and stop your bleeding, and restore your blood pressure, within an hour of your accident . . . then I can probably save you. I call that the golden hour." He said, "Our whole goal is to keep the patient alive. If you stop to diagnose, half your patients are dead. We treat before diagnosing."[18]

I believe there is a Golden Hour in which a response to a pastor's trauma is vital to his survival. What classifies as pastoral trauma? Trauma is an emotional response to a negative event.[19] There are multiple events that can have a negative mental and emotional impact on a pastor. A congregation split, the loss of an influential family, financial stress, negative criticism on social media, a confrontation, rejection, an attack on your integrity or your family, exposure to tragedy alongside members, just to name a few. Pastors regularly suffer from a combination of those issues, rather than just one. It is common for pastors to live under sustained pressure as a result of these negative events, and the pressure is crushing. All of that is in addition to any trauma the pastor has experienced in his personal life or family.

Everyone responds differently to trauma based on their emotional makeup. What is traumatic for me may not be traumatic for you. I can testify from experience, when someone has been over-exposed to trauma, it causes them to be more sensitive to negative events.

131

In my case, that usually resulted in an exaggerated response to a negative event.

Every pastor and every situation is different. There is no boiler plate response to a bleeding shepherd.

PASTORAL TRAUMA RESPONSE

I believe the answer to ministering to wounded pastors lies in this concept of the Golden Hour. Pastors who minister in prolonged extreme circumstances are at risk for Post-Traumatic Stress Disorder (P.T.S.D.). Timely response to mental and emotion trauma has been proven to minimize the effects of P.T.S.D. The suggested Golden Hour period is six hours.[20] Why? Research shows there is a six hour memory consolidation period after a traumatic event.[21]

Can churches and organizations respond to a bleeding shepherd's cry within the Golden Hour period? Can we reduce burnout, and rescue pastors from the battlefield? I believe we can. We are good at writing programs. We can map strategy on paper like no one else. We are professionals at rolling out initiatives. Our marketing is as convincing as a Madison Avenue advertisement. I believe we can put our effort into developing and implementing a practical strategy that will give pastors confidence. When pastors are assured we have their backs, they will acknowledge their wounds, embrace their healing, and minister more effectively.

My intention here is not to suggest all struggling pastors are suffering, or will suffer, from an anxiety disorder. I am merely trying to drive home this fact. We cannot keep allowing bleeding shepherds to die. We have a divine duty to act!

So, what should we do? I won't be so presumptuous as to suggest I have all the answers. On the contrary. However, I believe the same principles that are used to treat anxiety disorders (such as P.T.S.D.) can be used to help pastors.

Dr. Joseph Zohar, Director of Psychiatry at the Sheba Medical Center in Israel, suggests a simple outline of what to do for someone in the immediate aftermath of a traumatic event. He uses the acronym, E.R.A.S.E.

1. Reduce **E**xposure to stress;

2. **R**estore physiological needs;

3. Provide inform**A**tion/orient**A**tion;

4. Find a source of **S**upport;

5. Emphasize the **E**xpectation of returning to normal.[22]

When I read this during my research, it clicked for me. I did not originally set out to dive into the realm of mental and emotional health. However, on the journey to put my heart on paper, I discovered it is impossible for me to discuss my burnout without touching on my mental and emotional health as it relates to ministry. I won't spend a lot of time on this, but I want you to think about it.

Dr. Zohar's idea overlays effectively, in my opinion, as a Golden Hour response to pastoral trauma. I've substituted five key changes, in place of Dr. Zohar's acronym, and shared what they mean to me. Each one is an adaptation of the E.R.A.S.E. model. I believe these changes can be an effective emergent response.

1. Change the Environment

2. Change the Focus

3. Change the Sound

4. Change the People

5. Change the Goals

Change the Environment

Changing the environment reduces exposure to stress. When someone is wounded on the battlefield, the first priority is to get them out of harm's way. If necessary, a combat medic can treat a wounded soldier in the line of fire, but the optimal scenario is to get that soldier out of there, as soon as possible. (Remember, the Golden Hour doctrine is the basis for combat medicine.)

Changing the pastor's environment has the potential to reduce the immediate stress he is under. Once the environment has changed, and he no longer feels he's in danger, the walls that have been built up can begin to come down and healing can begin.

This is what happens in a pastoral sabbatical; the struggling pastor is temporarily removed from the environment that caused the stress. I'm an advocate of sabbaticals. I'm encouraged that organizations are beginning to widely embrace the emergency sabbatical idea. It's a start, but I believe we have a long way to go. Educating local congregations is key to the success of sabbaticals. The first one I took was three Sundays. Unfortunately, when I returned, a couple families had left the church. I contacted one of the gentlemen on the phone after I hadn't seen him for a week or two. He was not shy about telling me why his family was no longer attending. He sarcastically exclaimed, "I wish I could just take three weeks off whenever I wanted, and still get paid"

No matter what you say, some people will never get it.

Change the Focus

Change the focus away from the trauma and toward restoring physiological needs. After a traumatic event, it's natural to neglect personal needs, such as food and sleep. Your focus is elsewhere. Ministering to a pastor sometimes means removing the need for a pastor and family to have to worry about mundane daily tasks. Bringing food is a good way to help ease someone's burden, and it forces them to focus on their physiological needs. Getting the proper nutrition and sleep is key in managing stress.

This is the easiest part. Remember when I said everything we do revolves around food? We've mastered the art of providing meals for families grieving the loss of loved ones or families with new babies at home. When dealing with trauma, it's likely a pastor won't eat if you don't feed him.

Taking on this simple act of hospitality can change focus and help keep a family running smoothly.

Change the Sound

Changing the sound controls the nature of information. One of the greatest causes of stress to me, as a pastor, was what I was hearing. I allowed the negativity to get into my head. Changing the atmosphere and focus was not enough; I needed to change the sound. I got to a place where I didn't have the stomach for the toxicity of the people who wanted my ear. I was tired of feeling beaten down. I needed the noise to change to the sound of encouragement and hope.

One of the best things you can do for your pastor is to encourage him. That may be as simple as complimenting a sermon, or sending a text, just to say thank you. I can't tell you how many times I received a small note of appreciation from someone, and it made my day.

Sound makes the atmosphere. The mood in a room can change with the music being played. If the atmosphere is one of tension, change the sound.

Change the People

Changing the people organizes the pastor's source of support. When a pastor is struggling, he needs to be surrounded with friends and family. When you are hurting, friendly faces are a sight for sore eyes.

Since pastors are constantly under the pressure to perform, they need to be surrounded with people with whom they know they can be themselves. These are people around whom the pastor doesn't need to be the pastor, he can just focus on being human.

This is where the pastor needs to be connected with a mentor or spotter. The people with whom you associate are the people who have the most input and influence in your life. If I'm burning out, I want to be connected with a survivor, someone who has been through what I'm going through and has the scars to prove it. If they survived, they can show me the way out of the mess!

I need someone in the room who has been where I'm going. If you are surrounded by people who contribute more to the problem than the solution, you need to immediately change the people in your circle.

Change the Goals

Changing the goals reinforces the pastor's hope of returning to normal. Bleeding Shepherds need to be reminded that the trauma is temporary. We are often tempted to make long-term decisions based on temporary circumstances. Those experiencing trauma should not make any decisions at all. Surviving today includes not making decisions that will contaminate or delay your destiny.

Trauma can cause a pastor to be nearsighted in his goals. As I shared earlier, in the heat of my burnout, my goals were reduced to just trying to survive the day. My mind-set became, "I'll do anything I must do to survive today; I'll worry about tomorrow when it gets here." Imagine if that was your retirement investment strategy. Yeah. Enough said. It's a dangerous place to be.

A bleeding shepherd needs someone to help him keep his eyes on the bigger picture, to lift his gaze and be assured that the trauma is temporary, to be reminded that his decisions today will affect his tomorrow. He needs someone to look him in the eye and say, "Your destiny has not been affected by this deficit, nor has your calling been cancelled, nor will your vision be aborted. Your name is still on the list!"

GRACE TO RECOVER

The bottom line is, a bleeding shepherd needs those in authority over him, those around him, and those who serve under him, to give him Grace to recover.

Overseer, Elder, Bishop, Superintendent, please hear my heart. If a pastor under your leadership is burned out and headed for disaster, step in. Don't wait. Get under his arms, and give him Grace to recover. He doesn't need a manager. He needs a medic.

*"Instead of your shame you will receive a double portion,
and instead of disgrace you will rejoice in your inheritance.
And so you will inherit a double portion in your land, and
everlasting joy will be yours."*

(Isaiah 61:7)

CHAPTER ELEVEN

The Resurgence

RETURNING TO ME

I had not been myself for so long, I wasn't sure who "myself" was. For years, my identity had been shaped by what people expected of me and skewed by the pressure cooker of the pastorate. When I exited the ministry, those expectations and pressure weren't there anymore. All the labels I had been known by, preacher, pastor, bishop, leader, were gone now. Consequently, I went through an identity crisis.

The only label I had left was, officer. I knew how to be a good cop, but that is just what I did, not who I was. The only label I was left with I considered to be secondary to all the rest. Law enforcement had always been a diversion for me, not a career ambition.

I got into law enforcement as a chaplain back in the year 2000. The chief of police in the city where I pastored was a United Methodist pastor and gave me the opportunity to serve. I enjoyed serving the law enforcement community in ministry and it gave me a chance to get out of my box. I loved the law enforcement culture so much, I went to the police academy and obtained my peace officer certification. The rest, as they say, is history. Little did I know, the Lord would use this as my "brook in the wilderness".

In addition to an identity crisis, I had a relationship crisis. My relationship to many people in my life changed. When you go through a ministry failure, you feel as if you cease to exist to the people who only knew you according to your label. I want to be careful not to make a generalized statement here; I don't mean to suggest everyone abandoned me, but some people certainly did abandon me. It's a hard pill to swallow when people with whom you've had a long history start treating you as if they don't know you. It's kind of surreal. I discovered believers, even pastors, don't always reflect the grace and mercy of God.

Social media is a two-edged sword. It is a powerful tool when used correctly, but it is a curse if misused. Sometimes, it can just be annoying. I eventually had to spend some time away from social media because it was a constant reminder of who I wasn't anymore. It seemed every time I was on a social media outlet, I was confronted with post after post and picture after picture of pastors telling the world how wonderful their church is, how blessed they are to pastor there, and how large their crowds were getting. It made me ill, not that churches were growing and pastors were blessed, but that I could see right through all the masks. Oh, I used to be guilty of the same thing, portraying to the world a false sense of perfection in my life and ministry. What if pastors posted how they really feel on Monday morning? I suspect it would reveal the truth no one wants to talk about.

I stayed away from social media because it reminded me my circle had suddenly become much smaller. I was constantly reminded of my failures in contrast to everyone else's successes, whether real or just perceived.

DO YOU WANT TO BE WELL?

The Gospel of John, chapter five, tells the story of an invalid man at the pool of Bethesda whom Jesus healed. I love to take stories like this from scripture and break them down. When read prayerfully, these passages come to life and reveal prophetic truth we can apply directly to our lives.

"Now there is in Jerusalem near the Sheep Gate a pool, which in Aramaic is called Bethesda and which is surrounded by five covered colonnades. Here a great number of disabled people used to lie—the blind, the lame, the paralyzed. One who was there had been an invalid for thirty-eight years. When Jesus saw him lying there and learned he had been in this condition for a long time, he asked him, 'Do you want to get well?'" (Verses 1-6)

The pool of Bethesda is somewhat controversial for Bible scholars. I recently read an online article by Dr. Lizorkin-Eyzenberg, a Jewish Scholar who wrote, "A Jewish Gospel of John", which presents a historical basis for the pool of Bethesda being connected to an Asclepion, a temple to the Greco-Roman god of healing, Asclepius.

The article asserts the pool of Bethesda, which means, "house of mercy," is the place where diseased folks would come to seek the mercy of Asclepius. The article also asserts the first part of verse four, which describes an angel of the Lord stirring the water, is not found in the Latin Vulgate (one of the earliest translations of the Bible written around 200 A.D.) but was added by English translators to add clarification. In short, the pool of Bethesda was a place people came to seek a pagan god.[23]

I won't get into a theological debate over this view, as I'm not a Bible scholar, but there are some interesting arguments to support the theory. Do your research beginning with Dr. Eyzenberg's book. But, think about it for a moment. If this is true, it means the paralyzed, sick, and diseased were not waiting for Israel's God to come and heal them. Why is that important? Because it explains why the man at the pool was still there. He wasn't healed because he wasn't seeking the Healer!

The greater implication, though, is when he couldn't get to the Healer, the Healer came to him. Jesus learned the man had been infirm for thirty-eight years. He walked up to where he was lying and posed a question. The question, "Do you want to get well?" would seem to go without saying; who wouldn't want to be healed after almost four decades of paralysis? But, the man Jesus was addressing was lying in a hopeless place. He was lying in a place where it was rumored he could find his answer, but his answer never came. He had lost sight of his dream of ever being whole again and was just existing year after year, coping with this place of hopelessness. Jesus posed the question to reconnect the man with his dream.

The question goes beyond, "Do you want to get well?" Having an infirmity will attract dependency. When you're blind, you begin to depend on someone else to be your eyes. When you're deaf, you depend on someone else to be your ears. When you're lame, you depend on someone else to be your legs, etc. Consequently, the infirm can reach a place where they no longer have the need to depend on themselves for anything.

Not only does an infirmity attract dependency, it also can lead to an entitlement mentality. The mentality that I have a right to certain accommodations because I have an infirmity, could remove my desire to be whole, altogether. Therefore, when Jesus asked, "Do you want to get well?" He was asking, "Are you willing to lay down your dependency? Are you willing to relinquish your entitlements? Are you willing to give up your excuses? Are you willing to leave your crutches, your routines, your normal, and be whole? Would you rather work with two legs or continue begging with none?"

"Sir," the invalid replied, "I have no one to help me into the pool when the water is stirred. While I am trying to get in, someone else goes down ahead of me." (Verse 7)

Notice the man's response; it was not what one would've expected. He said, "I have no one to help me… every time I try to get in, someone else gets in my way." His response did not speak to his need; it spoke to his dependency.

I can almost hear the argument in his mind. "Jesus, I wouldn't still be in this spot if someone would have helped me get in the pool. Look at all these people around me. Their infirmities aren't as serious as mine. If they were more compassionate, I wouldn't still be in this place. If they weren't so selfish, I wouldn't be in this place. If someone would just help me, I wouldn't be in this place. I've tried and failed. I've done everything I know to do and nothing works. If I could just get a break, I wouldn't be here. It's not my fault I'm here, someone else is to blame."

The man at the pool was at the wrong place at the wrong time with the wrong people seeking the wrong answer. Jesus showing up is the only right thing in this equation. Nothing in this man's situation had changed between his infirmity and his healing except for presence of the Healer! The miracle didn't depend upon the barometer of his present. His location hadn't changed. His position hadn't changed. His surroundings hadn't changed. His view hadn't changed. The only thing that changed was his company.

Here's the thing. Jesus didn't ask the man why he was invalid or how he got that way; He asked if he wanted to be well. In other words, Jesus wasn't inquiring about his past, he was inquiring about his future.

The story of the man at the pool of Bethesda bears a stark resemblance to my personal experience. I wasn't an invalid (noun) in the sense I had a physical deficiency. I was invalid (adjective) because of what I had done, what I had been through. I believed my life and ministry had been invalidated by my past.

I had to answer the same question. Did I really want to be well? I was angry. I was bitter. I felt abandoned and betrayed by people who I thought would never leave me. I was busy pointing the finger and assigning blame. I was allowing my past to be my excuse to continue to fail.

When the Lord asked me if I wanted to be well, he wasn't asking me to justify my past or to offer some kind of excuse for my failures. He was aware of my deficiencies. He was asking me if I was willing to stop feeling sorry for myself, swallow my pride and learn to walk again. That very day, I released the heavy load I had been carrying. I took all the guilt, condemnation, anger, and bitterness that had been sitting on my shoulders and I left it at the altar. When I thought the game was over and I had lost, God sent the rain, delayed my game, and prepared me for another inning! That's when my resurgence began, and the course of the game changed completely!

Restoration always assumes there's a mess to fix. It's not a matter of whether God can or will restore you and make you whole. It's a matter of your willingness to let go of your dependencies, entitlements, justifications, and excuses and submit to the process.

There is a freedom that comes from releasing the need to reconcile your yesterday with your tomorrow. If you judge your ability to be used of God tomorrow by the failures that haunt you from yesterday, you'll lay at the place of infirmity without hope of ever being whole.

Do you want to be well? Once you answer that question, you'll be on your journey to restoration.

DOING WHAT COMES NATURALLY

Let me take you to another place in Scripture.

"As surely as the Lord your God lives," she replied, "I don't have any bread—only a handful of flour in a jar and a little olive oil in a jug. I am gathering a few sticks to take home and make a meal for myself and my son, that we may eat it—and die." (1 Kings 17:12)

If I were ever to publish the Wolf's Unauthorized Translation (WUT), I would put verse 12 first in this chapter. To grasp the reality of verses 8-11, you must understand the desperation of the widow in verse 12. In response to the Prophet Elijah, this woman reveals the desperation of her situation. She begins by telling him she doesn't have any bread. She admits to having something, but she is beyond hope that the little she has can make a difference in her

145

situation. She closes by revealing her expectations, that tomorrow will never come for her.

When you understand how serious her situation is, only then do you understand how ridiculous Elijah's request is.

"Then the word of the Lord came to him (Elijah): 'Go at once to Zarephath in the region of Sidon and stay there. I have directed a widow there to supply you with food.' So, he went to Zarephath. When he came to the town gate, a widow was there gathering sticks. He called to her and asked, 'Would you bring me a little water in a jar so I may have a drink?' As she was going to get it, he called, 'And bring me, please, a piece of bread.'" (Verses 8-11)

To put this in context, a widow had no income, no source, no status and no future. She was the opposite of what we believe "blessed" looks like. But what I love about this widow is, despite her deficiencies and limitations, she still showed up to gather sticks to prepare a meal just like any other day. She had a determination in her heart she would keep pressing until she had run out of options. She knew she had enough to make it one more meal, so she held on to that meager meal in a time of desperate hunger.

If you're experiencing the signs and symptoms of burnout, I want you to know that just merely showing up puts you in a position to prosper. If all you have is only enough for one more day, show up for that day! That could be the day your lack turns into plenty as it did for this widow!

I love that despite her desperation, she was willing to get Elijah some water without question. When someone is a servant, they can't shut it off. They will set aside their needs and wants to tend to someone else. They will overlook their pain to do what is in them.

As the widow turned to get Elijah some water, he called out to her, asking her to bring him some bread, also. This is where verse 12 comes in. She displayed her willingness to accommodate Elijah's first request, but now he was asking for something she wasn't sure she could provide. This is where she had to speak up and tell the prophet she didn't have any bread. Her condition was terminal. Her situation was dire. She essentially was saying to Elijah, "If you only knew what was going on in my house, you wouldn't be asking me for bread."

"Elijah said to her, 'Don't be afraid. Go home and do as you have said. But first make a small loaf of bread for me from what you have and bring it to me, and then make something for yourself and your son. For this is what the Lord, the God of Israel, says: 'The jar of flour will not be used up and the jug of oil will not run dry until the day the Lord sends rain on the land.'" (Verses 13-14)

Elijah wasn't being presumptuous as it may seem. He was only asking her to do what came naturally to her. He was asking her to walk in her gift of hospitality. Listen to what I'm about to say. When you're tired, weary, in pain, lonely, frustrated, betrayed, going without, and burned out, the one thing you can still do is keep walking in your gift. Showing up and walking in your gift may just put you in a position to prosper.

You will never be happy unless you're walking in your gift. When God created you to be and do a thing, He built into your divine DNA the need to be and do that thing. Your joy is tied to it. Your fulfillment is tied to it. You'll be miserable if you try to run from it. My resurgence required me to begin to walk in my gift again.

LET IT GO

First things first. I knew my journey to restoration included forgiving and asking for forgiveness. I had taken responsibility for my failure, but I had held a selected few responsible for contributing to my weakness. This isn't where I try to justify my feelings to you, they were what they were. This is where I tell you I let it go. I needed to forgive people I felt had left me for dead on the battlefield. I needed to forgive people who had the resources and the responsibility to help me, but I felt had failed to do so. Basically, I needed to forgive people whom I'm quite positive never lost any sleep over my burnout, but it wasn't for them. It was for me.

The hardest person to forgive was myself. I'm hard on myself. I'm my own worst critic. I beat myself up for a long time over my failures. Of the people with whom I was angry, I was most angry with myself. The reason I had such a hard time forgiving myself is because I couldn't justify my deficiencies. As long as I was blaming other people for my own mistakes, I didn't have to justify or reconcile anything because it wasn't my fault. It was easy to forgive others, but when I looked in the mirror and took responsibility, I suddenly saw the reflection of the man that needed my forgiveness the most, and I couldn't bring myself to do that. I had to live with the man in the mirror. I couldn't hide from him. I had to forgive him in order to face him and live with him.

Finally forgiving myself required me to conclude (with the help of the Holy Spirit) it was impossible for me to justify me, but it was entirely possible for Jesus to justify me. When I had that revelation, that's all it took. I left it in the hands of the Savior.

"For all have sinned and fall short of the glory of God, and all are justified freely by his grace through the redemption that came by Christ Jesus." (Romans 3:23-34)

I also needed to ask forgiveness. Of those whose name I had used in vain, I needed forgiveness. Of those whom I had hurt, let down, and disappointed, I needed forgiveness. Of those whom I had harbored anger and bitterness, I needed forgiveness. Of those whom had stood with me through it all, I needed forgiveness. Those were difficult conversations, but they brought a healing and freedom the enemy can never take away from me.

Resurgence and forgiveness go hand in hand. If you aren't ready to forgive and ask forgiveness, you aren't ready to be restored; you aren't ready to walk in your gift again. You must stop holding people responsible. You must turn your focus inward instead of pointing the finger. Take a look in the mirror, square your shoulders and tell yourself, "Let it go!" Whatever you are holding on to is holding on to you. It's time to let it go. You don't have to justify yourself, Jesus has already taken care of that.

You need to learn to use those three words. Regardless of how bad someone hurt you, what they said about you, the lies that were told about you, the assumptions that were made about you, how you feel people may have failed you. Let. It. Go. There is healing in those three little words. You will walk in a renewed freedom when you learn how to let it go. LET! IT! GO!

When you learn how to let it go, you will sleep better, your blood pressure will come down, your heart rate will normalize, you'll be slower to react to drama, your stress level will drop, you'll be happier, people will enjoy your company again. It will be the most freeing thing you will ever do aside from accepting Jesus. Trust me. Let it go.

When I finally let it go, The Lord began to release His favor. Within a seven-day period, I received invitations to preach, I received phone calls, text messages, Facebook messages, etc., from colleagues all over the country, each one independently joining the others with words of encouragement and affirmation. It was like my Heavenly Father had been preparing a surprise party for my return to myself! Through this outpouring of love, He proved to me that I had not been forgotten and my worth had not been reduced.

I finally realized that my destiny had not been dislodged.

WALKING IN MY GIFT

Here's the story of the day I went back to the pulpit after three years and fifteen days. A dear friend of mine pastors a church in Oklahoma. He had been dropping hints that his pulpit was open whenever I was ready. When I had not responded to the subtle invitation, he reached out one day and said, "Let's schedule this. Let's make it happen."

We set a date in January of 2017. On a Saturday, my wife and I drove to the Cincinnati/Northern Kentucky airport to get on a plane. We were flying into Dallas with a connection in Atlanta, then would drive two hours from Dallas to the church in small town Oklahoma. Our flight out of CVG was delayed due to a ground stop at ATL. There was a winter storm hitting Atlanta and there were no flights in or out. They changed our flight to another connecting airport, then that airport was placed on a ground stop. When we knew we had missed that connection, we went back to the ticket counter and asked them to find us a flight as close to Oklahoma as they could. They rerouted us to Houston, then on to Dallas from there. We were relieved to finally be leaving Cincinnati; we were beginning to think we weren't going to make it.

I knew what was going on. I was getting ready to have a major breakthrough in my resurgence. I was about to step back into my calling and the devil was angry. Truth is, my name was never taken off the list! The more difficult it became to get to my destination that day, the more I was convinced it was a divine appointment and the Lord would make sure I got there.

We finally boarded a plane and made it to Houston. We had a short wait, then boarded the plane for Dallas. If we could just get to Dallas, we could rent a car and be home free. Once we boarded, to our dismay, the captain came over the intercom to inform us there was some sort of delay in Dallas and we would be deplaning. We filed off the plane and began looking for another way. We contemplated renting a car and driving the rest of the way but it was too far.

In all my years of pastoring and traveling to preach, I had never experienced this much difficulty getting to my destination. I believed the enemy was working overtime to keep me away from this appointment, but I was even more determined than I was before. If I had any second thoughts, they were gone now. I was getting to Ada, Oklahoma if I had to hitchhike. Suddenly, they announced we were boarding the plane to Dallas yet again. Shortly thereafter, we were in the air and I knew everything was going to be all right. We landed in Dallas, rented a car and drove the rest of the way in.

The next morning, I stood in the pulpit for the first time in over three years and preached my heart out. The Lord moved that day. I'm not sure if anyone else received anything, but I did. That's the day my life snapped back into alignment with my calling and destiny. The feeling was indescribable.

REAFFIRMATION

One day, during a time of devotion I was reading the prayer of Jabez in 1 Chronicles 4:10.

"Jabez called on the God of Israel, saying, Oh that you would bless me indeed, and enlarge my coast, and that Your hand might be with me, and that You would keep me from evil, that it may not grieve me. And God granted him that which he requested." (AKJV)

Now, I've studied and preached this familiar passage many times, but on this occasion, I had a thought that had never occurred before. When it crossed my mind, I was revisited by tremendous guilt, condemnation, grief, and disappointment. As I read the words of Jabez' prayer, I thought, "I'm no longer worthy to pray that prayer." I hung my head and began to feel sorry for myself again, as I had done on so many occasions before. I had walked the treacherous path from burnout and failure to restoration and resurgence, and for the first time I had read something in scripture I thought no longer applied to me.

That night I made a God decision. I decided to go to a state camp meeting service for the first time in four years. I hadn't seen the people who would be in attendance in a long time; people who were once my circle. I walked into the service that night and something pivotal happened to me. I was continually greeted by person after person who expressed how glad they were to see me. It was like a family reunion. The ice was broken but the water was still a little chilly.

On that Tuesday night of camp meeting, I didn't care who the speaker was. For me it was about showing up. The Lord however, had arranged a divine appointment between the speaker and me and neither of us knew. Pastor Gary Taylor (now retired) was introduced and he took the stage. As special guests are accustomed to do, he spent a few minutes humbly honoring the leadership of the house and thanking the powers-that-be for giving him the opportunity.

Then he said, "Tonight, I want to talk about affirmation." From that very first word he had me and I hung on every word that followed.

That night the Lord reaffirmed me. He reminded me His blood is powerful enough for even me. He reminded me His calling on my life was not voided by my failure. He reminded me He knew who I was, He knew I wasn't perfect, He knew I was going to fail, but knowing, He called me anyway, He anointed me anyway, He appointed me anyway, and He loved me and forgave me anyway.

This reaffirmation was the final step in my resurgence. I knew the Lord had just renewed my commission and was sending me in a new direction.

"And we know that all things work together for good to those who love God, to those who are the called according to His purpose."

(Romans 8:28 NKJV)

CHAPTER TWELVE

The Mission

I began telling my story by asserting that God doesn't waste experiences. I believe that truth with everything in me because as horrible as my experience was, it wasn't wasted. I believe Romans 8:28.

"And we know that all things work together for good to those who love God, to those who are the called according to His purpose." (NKJV)

All things. As painful, heart-wrenching, damaging, and demoralizing as my history or your history may be, they qualify as "all things." They will always work together for good to those who love God, and are the called according to his purpose. Since God does not and will not rescind His calling, and His calling comes with the promise of Romans 8:28, God will honor that promise and turn your pain into your purpose and your mess into your mission.

I began my story with a dream and I will conclude with a dream. From the first to the last, I am convinced, no, convicted that the Lord gave me these dreams to bring revelation to the body of Christ. We need a revolution of restoration! I saved this one for last for a reason.

THE FINAL DREAM

In the dream I was in a building; I can only describe it as a metal building which bore a resemblance to an airplane hangar. It was empty and separated into two compartments by a large, transparent plastic sheet. It was sealed around the edges to make it airtight. There were two men in the hangar, one on each side of the plastic sheet. They were separated and isolated.

Of the two men, one was known to me and the other was not. The man I knew was a pastor. What is key in this dream is both men were suffocating. Not only was the plastic barrier between the men airtight, but the building was as well, and there was no airflow from the outside. Although I was there, in the building and able to breathe, I was completely unaffected by the atmosphere that seemed to be killing the men inside. I was compelled to come to their rescue.

As I was trying to help these men, I had a revelation. They weren't suffocating because they didn't have enough oxygen. The pastor was suffocated by his inability to share his message, and the other man was suffocated by his inability to hear the message. They were dying because they were unable to speak and receive the Word of God. I knew if I could somehow tear down the barrier, both men would live! I had to connect these men because one had the message that would save the other. I had to breathe life into that pastor!

In the dream, I was on the pastor's side of the hangar. He was trying to speak, but I couldn't understand what he was saying. I knew he was asphyxiating and quickly losing consciousness. I had to do something. I climbed up to the top of the hangar and found where the corner of the plastic sheet was sealed against the ceiling beam. I grabbed the edge and pulled on it as hard as I could until it tore away from the beam. I used my weight to pull the plastic sheet all the way down. I thought I had solved the problem, but it seemed to be too late. Both men were unconscious. I began performing CPR on the pastor just as the dream ended.

I awoke troubled, much like the other two dreams had left me. Only this time, I knew what the Lord was showing me. In the first two dreams I was the casualty. In this dream I was the medic. God had used this dream to illustrate my mission: to rescue dying pastors, bleeding shepherds.

There are several things about this dream I want to highlight.

Firstly, the pastor was experiencing what I call, "pastoral asphyxia." He was trying to speak life, but wasn't inhaling life. Imagine being able to exhale but when you inhale, there's no oxygen. Asphyxia. In my experience, it's very common for a pastor to spend all his energy pouring himself into others while neglecting his own well-being. When you are sealed off or isolated, you will eventually run out of oxygen. You must have a fresh supply to stay alive in ministry. People need to breathe in what you're breathing out. When you asphyxiate from the lack of God's life-giving breath, others will also asphyxiate from the lack of the life-giving Word. The bottom line is, in order to survive, the world must hear the message God has put in your mouth. For that reason, the enemy wants to suffocate you.

In law enforcement, we guard very carefully against something called, "positional asphyxia." This occurs when someone is restrained (such as in handcuffs and lying in the back seat of a police vehicle) in such a way that it prevents them from breathing properly. We are trained to prevent positional asphyxia by making sure a combative person is sitting up or on their side, when placed in the back seat, to keep their airway open. During transport, they must be constantly monitored.

Pastor, you must also guard against positional asphyxia. Listen carefully to what I'm about to say. Some of the stages of burnout that I shared in chapter 9, resistance, estrangement, disorientation, resentment, and detachment, can slowly restrain a pastor like the subtle squeeze of a python until you have no more breath. This is why it's so important to recognize and closely guard against these things. Maybe you feel as if you're in the grip of the python now. The only way to break its grip is to kill the python. There's a reason the scripture likens Satan to a serpent.

Secondly, the plastic barrier in the dream was transparent. There are pastors privately struggling who are visible, maintaining their stage presence, interacting with people, and going through the motions but there's not much life left in them. In my struggle, although preaching was the only thing that kept me going, it took all the energy I could muster to get up in front of people on Sunday. Some people are good at putting on a happy face when they're going through hell. I'm not one of them. It was difficult for me to be public while trying to hide the pain of my struggle.

Remember the second dream I shared? I was in a room full of people, bleeding and dying but no one noticed. That is a reflection of the pulpit relationship between pastor and congregation. A bleeding shepherd will do his best to hide his injury in the pulpit, or public life. Why? Because he is trying to hold together what he feels is left of his ministry. If he loses his ministry, he feels he has nothing left.

Here's where I give you something critical to think about. If bleeding shepherds do their best to hide their wounds, why was I not hiding my mortal head wound in that second dream? Why was I walking through the waiting room filled with people trying to alert someone, anyone, to my desperate need for help? Why did I want someone, anyone, to see my fatal vulnerability? My answer may startle you. Then again, you may relate.

When I sought the help of those with the resources and responsibility to help me, I felt I was ignored. I felt abandoned on the battlefield. I felt betrayed by those who should've had my back. These people were represented by the doctors and nurses I encountered in the second dream. When they failed to treat my wounds, I came to a place where I no longer cared who saw me bleeding. I didn't expect to live, so I laid down everything I worked for and gave up. That's where my private struggle became public.

When a pastor's struggle becomes public, it isn't the beginning of the struggle, it's the end. Usually, it becomes public because of a failure. When it becomes public, people begin talking, gossiping, pontificating, and assuming they know the story. Every time it's told it becomes bigger and more scandalous. The truth is, the gossipers only know what is public. Only a select few people close to that pastor know the truth.

The truth is, he's been to hell and back. He's fought battles no one has ever seen. He's questioned his own faith. He's doubted his very calling. He's cried himself to sleep countless nights. He has no dignity left. He has lost his self-respect. He has beaten himself up

159

relentlessly. He's exhausted, starving, thirsty, battered, scarred, afraid, and alone. The truth is, he's been harder on himself than anyone will ever be on him, and the people with the log in their own eyes should stop considering the pastor's splinter "news."

Now, back to the final dream.

Thirdly, the pastor was alone. Looking back at my experience, I was alone because I was isolating myself, not because I wasn't loved and supported. If it were not for a select few men of God who saw me alone and asphyxiating and pulled down the barrier, I wouldn't have received my restoration. I'm thankful for faithful comrades who never left me, never treated me differently, never rescinded their affection of me. They are true friends. They are my ambassadors of restoration. My combat medics. I owe them my life. They know who they are.

Fourthly, my dream ended before the story ended. This troubled me. I was administering CPR to the pastor when the dream ended. What does this mean? This is what the Lord said to me. "The dream ended before your work was finished so I could give you the revelation that your work is not finished. When you awoke, the story wasn't over because *your* story is not over, and the story is not over for the bleeding shepherds to whom I will send you. I have assigned you as a medic to wounded pastors."

This is how Resurgence was born.

RESURGENCE IS BORN

The Lord gave me a miraculous resurgence. With it came a divine mandate to reach out to others who need a resurgence. When I went back to the pulpit in January of 2017, the Lord instructed me to put this name on the ministry. It would mark my mission.

In January of 2018, I prayerfully approached eight Godly men and asked them to partner with me in ministry. They now serve as the Resurgence Board of Elders and, as of October 2018, Resurgence became a non-profit corporation.

Resurgence is more than just a name, it's a cadence. It's a battle cry. I pray every wounded pastor hears the cry, while they lay feeling helpless and alone on the battlefield, as a message of hope.

If you forget everything I said, remember this. What I went through could've killed me, but it didn't. Neither, will it kill you.

The Lord has called me to prophesy Resurgence over your life and ministry. You thought you were left for dead, but you are going to rise again into life. You thought you would never again be effective, but you are going to rise again into relevance. You believed you were forgotten, but you are going to rise again into prominence. It's time for your comeback!

Your ministry will survive your failure. God refuses to take back His calling and I refuse to leave a man behind. You can be restored!

About The Author

Jeff Wolf began preaching at the age of fifteen. He spent more than two decades of ministry in one of the world's foremost full gospel organizations. His ministry assignments included national evangelist, lead pastor, denominational state executive leadership, as well as numerous boards, committees, and commissions.

After struggling with burnout and its aftermath, Jeff resigned the ministry in early 2014, and plummeted into a season of deep despondency. In the face of challenging odds, Jeff sought the counsel of a core of trusted Godly comrades, who admonished, loved, and nurtured him back to health. Jeff was restored to the ministry and began a journey to reach out to bleeding shepherds.

From his miraculous restoration, Jeff founded Resurgence, a nonprofit corporation that endeavors to raise awareness and foster prevention of the crippling epidemic of pastoral burnout. Jeff travels the nation, encouraging and mentoring pastors, on a mission to mitigate the casualties of ministry.

Jeff has committed to revealing his scars to be a living witness that your ministry can survive your failure.

RESURGENCEINC

Visit our website for more information:

www.resurgenceinc.org

Endnotes

1   Muskat, Carrie. "Cubs Win World Series after 108 Years Waiting." MLB.com, 3 Nov. 2016, www.mlb.com/cubs/news/cubs-win-world-series-after-108-years-waiting/c-207995060.

2   Doolittle, Bradford. "The Rain-Delay Meeting That Changed Cubs History." ESPN, ESPN Internet Ventures, 3 Nov. 2016, www.espn.com/blog/chicago/cubs/post/_/id/42846/the-rain-delay-meeting-that-changed-cubs-history.

3   Gibson, Mel, director. Hacksaw Ridge. Cross Creek Pictures, Demarest Films, Pandemonium (as Pandemonium Films), Permut Presentations, Vendian Entertainment, 2017.

4   Dickens, Charles, et al. A Tale of Two Cities. Pearson Education Ltd., 2008. Chapter 1.

5   Krejcir, R J. "Statistics on Pastors." Into Thy Word. Teaching People How to Study the Bible, Francis A. Schaeffer Institute of Church Leadership Development, www.intothyword.org/apps/articles/?articleid=36562.

6   Treffeisen, Beth. "The Tricky Work of Guiding Tankers into Boston Harbor - The Boston Globe." BostonGlobe.com, The Boston Globe, 11 June 2015, www.bostonglobe.com/magazine/2015/06/11/the-tricky-work-guiding-tankers-into-boston-harbor/pUrp9LLaNOg1ity5Oh3XVP/story.html.

7   Scott, Tony, director. Crimson Tide. Hollywood Pictures Home Video, 1995.

8   Marshall, Samuel L. A. Bastogne the Story of the First 8 Days in Which the 101. Airborne Division Was Closed within the Ring of German Forces. Zenger, 1979. Chapter 14.

9   Enochs, Tim. "One Degree Off Course." Uncommon Influence, www.uncommoninfluence.com/one-degree-off-course/.

10   Garner, Todd, et al. Paul Blart, Mall Cop. Sony Pictures Entertainment, 2009.

11   "Visual Acuity: What Is 20/20 Vision?" American Optometric Association, www.aoa.org/patients-and-public/eye-and-vision-problems/glossary-of-eye-and-vision-conditions/visual-acuity.

12   Wikipedia contributors. "Average." Wikipedia, The Free Encyclopedia. Wikipedia, The Free Encyclopedia, 31 Dec. 2018. Web. 18 Feb. 2019.

13   Stone, Perry. Perry Stone Ministries. 14 Apr. 2018, www.facebook.com/perrystonevoe/photos/the-anointing-attracts-attacks-perry-stone/1894525327248848/.

14   Wikipedia contributors. "Spatial disorientation." Wikipedia, The Free Encyclopedia. Wikipedia, The Free Encyclopedia, 11 Feb. 2019. Web. 18 Feb. 2019.

15   Lambert, Bruce (November 1, 1991). "Dr. R. Adams Cowley, 74, Dies; Reshaped Emergency Medicine". The New York Times.

16   Wikipedia contributors. "Golden hour (medicine)." Wikipedia, The Free Encyclopedia. Wikipedia, The Free Encyclopedia, 2 Jan. 2019. Web. 19 Feb. 2019.

17   Schoettler, Carl. "Dr. R Adams Cowley, Shock-Trauma Pioneer, Dies." Baltimoresun.com, 26 Oct. 2018, www.baltimoresun.com/news/bs-xpm-1991-10-28-1991301102-story.html.

18   Schoettler, Carl. "Dr. R Adams Cowley, Shock-Trauma Pioneer, Dies." Baltimoresun.com, 26 Oct. 2018, www.baltimoresun.com/news/bs-xpm-1991-10-28-1991301102-story.html.

19   "Trauma." American Psychological Association, American Psychological Association, www.apa.org/topics/trauma.

20   Kent, Martha Whalen., et al. The Resilience Handbook Approaches to Stress and Trauma. Routledge, 2014. Page 304.

21   Greenwald, Ricky. "Preventing Traumatic Memory Consolidation." Trauma Institute, 4 May 2015, www.childtrauma.com/blog/preventing-consolidation/.

22   Zohar, Joseph. "Window of Opportunity - the Golden Hours of Stress-Related Disorders." Does Natural Selection Favour Depression? | Progress In Mind, 10 Mar. 2017, progress.im/en/content/window-opportunity-golden-hours-stress-related-disorders.

23   Dr. Lizorkin-Eyzenberg. "The Pool of Bethesda as Greek Asclepion." Israel Study Center, 6 Feb. 2018, israelstudycenter.com/was-bethesda-jewish-or-pagan/.